CONCISE
LINCOLN
LIBRARY

—

EDITED BY RICHARD W. ETULAIN,
SARA VAUGHN GABBARD, AND
SYLVIA FRANK RODRIGUE

FRANK J. WILLIAMS

Lincoln as Hero

Southern Illinois University Press
Carbondale and Edwardsville

Frontispiece: Vignette portrait of Abraham Lincoln
taken by T. P. Pearson in 1858. As a candidate for the
U.S. Senate, Lincoln saw his political star ascend ow-
ing to the national renown earned from his debates
with Stephen A. Douglas and from his support of free
labor. Courtesy of the Frank and Virginia Williams
Collection of Lincolniana.

The Concise Lincoln Library has been made possible
in part through a generous donation by the Leland E.
and LaRita R. Boren Trust.

ISBN 978-0-8093-3217-5

Book Club Edition

To my law clerks, who have endured and evolved
and who are all emerging heroes

CONTENTS

ILLUSTRATIONS

PREFACE

Since it declared its independence from England in 1776, America has looked for heroes to lead the country and its people. The story of America and its quest for independence, justice, and equality is the story of heroic individuals. Fortunately, however, this heroism was not so prevalent that it would confirm the country's fears of another monarchy.

When we think of a hero, we think of the person who is called upon to do extraordinary things. We think of the person whose spirit rises above adversity in the name of justice and right. We think of the person who not only strives for social change but also seeks to inspire people to accept change. Abraham Lincoln, the self-educated prairie boy who picked himself up by the bootstraps and made an enduring name for himself, is just such a person. Lincoln was clear and confident in his belief that individuals should live free from tyranny, terrorism, and tumult. Though abhorring war, Lincoln came to realize that the nation could not endure half slave and half free. At that realization, he did not equivocate or timidly talk of peace. Rather, he committed all resources—political, economic, and human—to the eradication of inequality.

Heroes emerge from the circumstances they are presented. Theodore Roosevelt once said when reflecting on Abraham Lincoln, "A man has to take advantage of his opportunities but the opportunities have to come. If there is not the war, you don't get the great general; if there is not the great occasion, you don't get the great statesman; if Lincoln had lived in times of peace, no one would know his name now."[1] Likewise, historian Alan Brinkley once noted, "Great presidents are products not just of their own talents and ambitions but of the circumstances they inherit."[2]

Heroes often embody the principles of great leadership: hope, confidence, and unshakable moral courage. A hero is someone who can distinguish between and act upon the essential and the peripheral—between what must be done and what is merely desirable. For Lincoln, this meant all else had to be sacrificed to the overwhelming necessity of holding the Union together behind the principles of the Declaration of Independence. A hero is someone who embodies courage and strength to stand against political pressures and public perception and who has the ability to stay the course even when standing alone, who is not afraid to do what he or she believes in, and who will stand up for what is right. It is strong will and persistence that inspire us and flaws and imperfections that allow us to identify even further with the hero. In the words of the late actor Christopher Reeve, "a hero is an ordinary individual who finds the strength to persevere and endure in spite of overwhelming obstacles."[3] Lincoln eloquently professed the significance he placed on honor and character—in himself and in others—in one sentence: "I desire to conduct the affairs of this administration that if at the end, when I come to lay down the reins of power, I have lost every other friend on earth, I shall at least have one friend left, and that friend shall be down inside me."[4]

Willpower is the most important of all qualities in public life. A politician can have immense intelligence and other virtues, like the ability to communicate, but if will is lacking, a hero will not emerge. Lincoln had it in abundance. He saw the Civil War to a successful conclusion regardless of the sacrifice, damage, and blow-back engendered by it. As Lincoln's leadership demonstrates, mere flashes of will are not enough. The will must be inextricably linked to resolution, a determination to see the cause through at all costs. There are dark days in every venture, however just. One aspect of pertinacity is patience. Another is a certain primitive doggedness. Lincoln knew this in his long and often agonizing struggle during the Civil War.

Genuine heroes are realists, and Lincoln was the quintessential realist. He was a realist in his understanding that to save the Union, he must emancipate the slaves—not only for political or moral reasons but also for military objectives, including the vast resource that slaves, after they were liberated, could provide in the army and navy. Lincoln was a realist in understanding that in order to "preserve the institutions of this country—those institutions which have made us free," he needed to build a formidable citizen army.[5] He was realistic in understanding the concept of mission and how to achieve an objective. When politicians protested against a new draft in the midst of the presidential campaign because it might cost him the election, he demanded, "What is the presidency worth to me if I have no country?"[6] He was realistic about public support, remarking wisely in one crisis, "I do not need sympathy nearly so much as I need success."[7]

Most heroes—and Lincoln is no exception—are looked up to as heroic in part because of their ability to communicate. The value of possessing a few basic ideas that are genuine and workable is enormously enhanced if the leader can put them across with simplicity. Though George Washington lacked skill in plausible speechmaking, Lincoln was not only a great orator for a set occasion but also someone whose everyday remarks carried enormous power. Because he wrote his letters and state papers to be read aloud and widely published, he enhanced his communication with his constituents. History also teaches that an admired hero who can make the public laugh is likely to have a strong and lasting hold on its affections. Abraham Lincoln loved irony. He often achieved an effect with jokes where mere oratory would not work.

Heroes are successful not only by the standards of their own time but also by their achievements that transcend their era and resonate throughout history. Historian Paul Johnson observes, "Anyone is a hero who has been widely, persistently over long periods, and enthusiastically regarded as heroic by a reasonable person, or even an unreasonable one."[8] The circumstances of Lincoln's life and his legacy, time and again, transcend his era. And it is because of this legacy that the world still talks about Lincoln and his greatness. A certain magnanimity makes a leader and statesman a hero. It is a virtue that makes one warm to its possessor and love Lincoln because he had magnanimity to an unusual degree—in forgiving the South and those who fought for it in order "to bind up the nation's wounds."[9] It was part of his inner being. To paraphrase Lincoln biographer Carl Sandburg, millions of people outside the United States also take him for their own.

LINCOLN AS HERO

INTRODUCTION

I n her *Team of Rivals: The Political Genius of Abraham Lincoln*, historian Doris Kearns Goodwin describes a 1908 exchange between Leo Tolstoy and tribal people living in a remote mountain village of Eurasia.[1] During that visit, at the tribal chief's request, the Russian literary legend regaled his isolated audience with stories of the world's great leaders, from Alexander to Caesar to Napoleon.

But it was another leader the chief and his tribe most wanted to hear about, Goodwin writes, the man from the West who "spoke with a voice of thunder; he laughed like the sunrise and his deeds were as strong as a rock. . . . [H]is name was Lincoln." Tolstoy obliged them with stories of Lincoln's modest childhood, physical strength, and ultimate influence, amazed that the Lincoln myth flourished even there. The writer, a Lincoln admirer on the order of Walt Whitman and Carl Sandburg, later predicted that it would only grow with passing years: "We are still too near his greatness. But after a few centuries more our posterity will find him considerably bigger than we do. His genius is still too strong and too powerful for common understanding, just as the sun is too hot when its light beams directly on us."[2]

The author of *War and Peace* got it just right. Today, the sixteenth president lingers at the heart of the American imagination as no other figure in the nation's history, popping up in contemporary culture with a frequency only Jesus Christ rivals.

Of the thousands of books about him over the years, one popular recent volume studies his melancholy; another, the manhunt to find

Lincoln's killer. Memorization of the Gettysburg Address remains an elementary school rite. Steven Spielberg, at this writing, is producing a film based on the Goodwin biography *Team of Rivals*.

Lincoln scholars now say that the lanky lawyer's staying power renders traditional explanations for it insufficient.

The secret of Lincoln's endurance has as much to do with subtle virtues like his wisdom, compassion, and abiding goodness. His tenderness as a father, his patience in a difficult marriage, his stalwartness as a friend, his magnanimity in bitter defeat, and humility and grace in victory represent Lincoln's more subtle virtues. In short, Lincoln is one of the few figures of history who is magnified by intense scrutiny, not diminished by it.

Abraham Lincoln's leadership can only be understood by grasping the challenges he faced. Those challenges included not only the Confederacy and its military but also a starkly divided Northern electorate and public opinion. Lincoln had to win a war at home as well as one against a more obvious enemy.

Thought to be the first modern president for a host of reasons, Lincoln faced conflicts, mistakes, miscalculations, and competing values everywhere he turned. He invented a concept of presidential war powers that the U.S. Supreme Court later rebuked. Against a complicated political backdrop, he issued the Emancipation Proclamation, citing it as a military, not a moral, necessity. He conducted a balancing act between abolitionists and Border State moderates, between radicals and conservatives, and struggled with a parade of generals over military strategy.

As scholar James MacGregor Burns points out in his seminal book *Leadership*, "[W]ars, depression, domestic unrest, [and] great moral issues . . . posed the most urgent questions of value and purpose for pragmatic politicians, however much they have sought to evade them."[3]

Lincoln could not evade the realities of his time, and we understand his leadership by examining how he faced them. He can be praised as a pragmatic yet deeply principled leader.

In the 1850s, Lincoln saw a fundamental moral conflict looming between slavery and freedom. Out of that conflict, he said, the nation would become either all slave or all free. His political nemesis Stephen A. Douglas, on the contrary, saw no such conflict and imagined that the white man's democracy of the time could preserve a peaceful consensus on the slavery issue.

This book attempts to reach a disinterested judgment on key features of Lincoln's presidential leadership: his vision, strategic command, political management, and techniques as a communicator.

Almost all leaders want to be the brilliant visionary in a time of crisis—the ones who see the situation clearly, make the bold plans, and deliver the faithful to their side. It almost never works out that way. The historian Henry Adams concludes, "In all great emergencies . . . everyone was more or less wrong."[4] Abraham Lincoln did not feel like a heroic leader: "I claim not to have controlled events, but confess plainly that events have controlled me."[5] In real crises, the successful leaders are usually the ones who cope best with ignorance and error—as did President Lincoln.

Leaders who are heroic while working out their personal problems also respond to the needs of others. And followers come to identify leaders with their needs, sometimes with their hopes, sometimes with their fears and insecurity.

Lincoln was particularly sensitive to the needs of others. He made himself available almost daily to mothers whose sons were lost in war, businessmen with special problems, and politicians—hundreds who trekked through the White House to unburden themselves and to transfer their needs to the president. After hearing from a wide variety of people, he had a secretary write to the heads of departments about the matters brought to him. Though often exhausted, Lincoln refused to reduce the time allotted for his "public opinion baths" when Senator Henry Wilson of Massachusetts advised him to cut back his access to the public, the president responded, "They don't have much, they don't get but little, and I must see them."[6]

Heroism, as with leadership, is a complicated and sometimes emotional issue. What these heroes have in common is what their anti-types lack—an ability to benefit from a reciprocal engagement between two wills, those of the leader and the follower. Abraham Lincoln had to consider his constituents. So he asserted "the superior position assigned to the white race"; had he not done so he would never have been in a position to do any leading at all.[7]

Abraham Lincoln's goodness is at the heart of his heroic nature, a generosity of spirit most appreciated by those closest to him. "No man is ever a hero to his valet," someone has opined, but look at the way Abraham Lincoln's White House secretaries John Nicolay and John Hay felt about their boss. They loved him, and they were with him day by day.

Not that there have not been regular attempts to demythologize the rail-splitter from the stove-pipe hat. In fact, some have argued in recent decades that Lincoln was as much white supremacist as emancipator. That view derives largely from Lincoln's stated belief that freed slaves might be better off back in Africa and from his statements in the Lincoln-Douglas debates of 1858, when he said he had "no purpose to introduce political and social equality between the white and black races" or of "making voters or jurors of negroes, nor or qualifying them to hold office, nor to intermarry."[8]

Although his racial attitudes are grossly antiquated by today's standards, historians point out that Lincoln was a cutting-edge progressive in his time. Respected black abolitionist Frederick Douglass said Lincoln was "the first great man that I talked with in the United States freely, who in no single instance reminded me of the difference between himself and myself, of the difference of color."[9]

Lincoln has also been regularly criticized for his suspension of the writ of habeas corpus during the Civil War, for his management of his field generals, and the length of time it took him to issue the Emancipation Proclamation. Scholars also attempt to tease out titillating aspects of his personal life such as tales of his time spent with prostitutes, during which he may even have contracted syphilis. Current speculation about Lincoln's sexuality is fueled by the fact that for four years he shared the same bed in Springfield, Illinois, with his best friend, Joshua Speed—though the practice was common in that time and place.

But objections to the Lincoln legend have yet to gain traction, largely because of the sort of wisdom and magnanimity of the man. After all, how many leaders would, as Lincoln did after his victory

Memorial print for Lincoln, H. H. Lloyd, New York, New York, n.d. The hero Lincoln was not recognized by all during his lifetime, but most, including political opponents and people in the South, recognized his goodness and their loss after his assassination. Courtesy of the Frank and Virginia Williams Collection of Lincolniana.

in 1860, invite into his cabinet men who in previous years had often treated him with condescension or cruelty?

When Abraham Lincoln was elected president, it was widely doubted that he possessed the necessary background and experience to be a successful leader. Lincoln had almost no formal schooling. One of the tools it was thought he conspicuously lacked was a facility for writing. But Lincoln's unsuspected literary ability worked to his advantage as a hidden asset, enabling him to communicate effectively with his constituents and to persuade them to accept difficult measures and decisions.

"Public sentiment is everything," Lincoln said at one of his debates with Senator Douglas.[10] He realized that to change public opinion demanded more than rhetorical devices. One of the things that accounts for Lincoln's greatness was an exacting literary craft. His important writings went through many revisions as his aim was to create "the impassioned tone that comes from sincerity and conviction."[11]

It was almost as if he knew that his words would resonate throughout time: "Fellow citizens, we cannot escape history. . . . The fiery trial through which we pass, will light us down, in honor or dishonor, to the latest generation."[12] Crafted to meet the immediate contingencies of the Civil War, Lincoln's writings continue to be read and to affect the nation's sense of itself, of its history and his heroism.

The work that follows will demonstrate that Lincoln is a hero not only by the standards of his day but also by today's standards as well. In doing so, this book examines Lincoln as a hero anecdotally through six subtopics: Lincoln's rise as a young man, his training and experiences as a lawyer, his introduction into politics, his growing understanding of military tactics and leadership, his handling of "extraconstitutional measures," and the Emancipation Proclamation.

THE PRAIRIE BOY FROM
MIDDLE-OF-NOWHERE, USA

A hero may emerge in myriad forms. Heroes may be rich or poor, famous or inconspicuous, but if there's one common thread that unites so many American heroes, it is that they are grounded by their humble beginnings. Abraham Lincoln is one of the finest examples of the American dream. As someone who used his education as a means to rise from humble beginnings to become America's greatest president, he exemplifies what Historian Gabor S. Boritt calls the American "right to rise."[1] Driven by an unquenchable thirst for knowledge and fueled further by a complex that he was somehow intellectually inadequate—an "underdog" syndrome of sorts—Lincoln tirelessly committed himself to self-education. The fruit of his labor was the development of an intellect, independence of thought, and strength of character that fortified him to meet the unprecedented challenges that lay ahead of him.

Lincoln's formal education during his young life was extremely limited and irregular. Due to his agricultural chores, itinerant teachers, and the relative distance of the local frontier schoolhouse from the family cabin, Lincoln attended school sporadically. All told, Lincoln spent what amounted to roughly one year in so-called blab schools. In these aptly named schools, all of the students sat together in a one-room log cabin and learned by repeating their lessons out loud. The teachers themselves were seldom educated beyond a basic proficiency in reading, writing, and mathematics. It is understandable, therefore, why, in response to an 1858 legislative questionnaire, Lincoln wrote "defective" in the line marked "education."[2] This lack of formal education always bothered him and influenced Mary Todd Lincoln's decision to enlist private tutors for their sons and preparatory school for Robert so he could attend Harvard College. Nevertheless, Lincoln cautioned Robert about Harvard: "You should learn more than I ever did, but you will never have so good a time."[3] Judging from the photo in Harvard's Houghton Library Collection of a casual Robert in the Smoker's Club, one would have to disagree.

Still, the blab schools were important in that they provided Lincoln with an educational foundation upon which he could build. Once he had learned how to spell through practice and repetition, he progressed to reading and writing with the help of *Dilworth's Spelling Book*—a constant companion during his youth. His thirst for knowledge was so great that he would read anything he could get his hands on. Childhood friend Nathaniel Grigsby observed, "Whilst other boys were idling away their time Lincoln was at home studying hard."[4] He also would copy down and rewrite passages that particularly struck him so that he could commit them to memory.[5]

Reading almost entirely occupied his spare time, including the brief breaks between his labors. In fact, his overzealousness sometimes got the better of him, and he would neglect his work in favor of reading, which drew the ire of his father, Thomas, along with an occasional beating.[6] As was customary on the frontier, Lincoln's wages belonged to his father in return for raising and maintaining Lincoln and teaching him to farm.[7]

Books were so scarce in the Indiana frontier that Lincoln found himself reading the same ones over and over again. Besides serving as a useful exercise in memorization, the repetition allowed Lincoln to delve deeply into the books and to master their language and meaning. Among his favorite titles were *Aesop's Fables*, the King James version of the Bible, *The Pilgrim's Progress* by John Bunyan, and *The Life of George Washington* by Parson Weems.[8] Each book played an influential role in Lincoln's education. Weems's *Washington*, although hyperbolic, provided Lincoln a hero, along with the men of the colonial army, to whom he could aspire, and

Pilgrim's Progress served as an illustration of man's potential to better himself.

The Bible and *Aesop's Fables* were particularly influential in cultivating Lincoln's ethics. One need look no further than his speeches to see how significantly these sources influenced his thinking and discourse. For example, his famous house-divided speech, in which he argued against the divisiveness of the continuation of slavery in the southern states, derives obviously from the Gospels and from the tale of "The Lion and the Four Bulls" in *Aesop's Fables*. Quoting scripture, Lincoln warned, "A house divided against itself cannot stand."[9] The tale of "The Lion and the Four Bulls" emphasized the point in Lincoln's mind. In this parable, the lion was not able to attack the four bulls when they stood together but was able to kill them individually after they had separated from each other.

Lincoln also read William Grimshaw's *History of the United States*, which attacked the institution of slavery and encouraged the reader: "Let us not only declare by words, but demonstrate by our actions, that 'all men are created equal.'"[10] Lincoln knew as a youth that slavery was morally wrong; Grimshaw's book taught him that slavery also was incompatible with America's founding principles, as expressed in the Declaration of Independence.

As a teenager, Lincoln progressed to more-challenging pieces of literature, including Shakespeare and poetry, particularly the work of Robert Burns. He also began to develop his own voice, penning essays and poems that demonstrated how much he had learned from authors and poets and evidenced his own wit and thoughtful attitudes on a variety of topics.[11]

Perhaps the most important role that school played in young Lincoln's life was that it engrained in him a self-confidence and self-awareness of his leadership potential. As was evidenced by his dominance in school spelling bees, Lincoln surpassed his fellow students in intelligence and eloquence. Because he was generous in sharing his knowledge and told fascinating stories, Lincoln became quite popular and well respected among his peers.[12] His schooling thus provided him with a strong foundation of interpersonal skills and a sense of confidence required of all good leaders.

Lincoln also learned many important life lessons from his family and upbringing in southern Indiana. Most significant, he learned how to accept hardship. In the winter of 1816, when Abraham was just seven years old, the family moved from Kentucky to the virtually uninhabited wilderness of Pigeon Creek, Indiana. Together they survived the harsh winter in a hastily built and uninsulated log cabin, subsisting primarily on deer meat. The family also faced peril from the surrounding forest, which was populated with bears, panthers, wolves, and other predators. Although he was just a young boy, his father enlisted him to hunt and to perform the grueling task of clearing land with an ax (25).

Two years later at nine years old, Abraham suffered great personal tragedy when his mother, Nancy, died of "milk sickness"—brucellosis—which she, like many other unsuspecting members of the Pigeon Creek community, contracted from drinking the milk of cows that had grazed on the poisonous white snakeroot plant. Nancy's death was a harsh lesson for Abraham in the fragility of life (26).

Fortunately, he soon became close with his stepmother, Sarah Rush Johnston Lincoln, who encouraged his education and considered him to be the best boy she had ever known, even compared to her own biological sons (28). His stepmother no doubt contributed to Abraham's education by bringing to the Lincoln cabin a small collection of books, which he readily and thoroughly digested, including *Arabian Nights*, *Robinson Crusoe*, and William Scott's *Lessons in Elocution*.[13]

Sarah was not the last woman from whom Lincoln learned. Later, his well-educated wife, Mary Todd, also played a significant edifying role in enlarging his life. Because Mary had a discerning mind and was intellectually capable of understanding complex questions of public importance that her husband was presented, she was able to offer him her perspective and advice. Additionally, Mary's ambitious spirit served to spur Lincoln forward. She quickly envisioned great things for him and no doubt aided his career by stirring him rather than simply playing the role of an obedient wife.[14]

Ironically, some relatives assumed that Lincoln was not very bright because it took him a long time to learn something. His stepmother, however, was more perceptive: "He must understand everything—even to the smallest thing—minutely and exactly. . . . [H]e would then repeat it over to himself again and again—sometimes in one form and then in another and when it was fixed in his mind to suit him he . . . never lost that fact or his understanding of it."[15] In fact, as a child, Lincoln would often lie awake at night trying to decipher conversations between adults that he had heard during the day. The thoroughness and determination with which Lincoln approached his early education explains his success later in life when he tackled far more complex subjects like law, politics, and the art of war.

Lincoln was not receptive to his father's decision to settle his family on the Indiana frontier, which lacked intellectual pursuits. Abraham looked down on what he viewed as his father's lack of ambition and complacency with his status in life as a manual laborer. As writer Fred Kaplan sums up, in many ways Thomas Lincoln taught his son by negative example.[16]

Abraham did, however, have his father to thank for ingraining in him, almost from birth, remarkable storytelling skills and a disfavor for slavery. One subject that Abraham cared little about learning was his family background. He once remarked, "I don't know who my grandfather was, and I am much more concerned to know what his grandson will be."[17] While the comment is, to a degree, irreverent, it is also indicative of a "fire in the belly" of a self-made man determined to achieve greatness.

Even from a young age, Lincoln demonstrated an independent streak. Although he hunted as a young child, Lincoln grew to detest killing and had stopped altogether by the time he was eight years old. He even admonished other neighborhood children for torturing animals and wrote an essay against cruelty to animals. His argument that "an ant's life was to it as sweet as ours to us" can be simply understood and not easily disputed.[18]

Lincoln also chose to join the relatively small Whig Party over the more dominant Democratic Party. He never joined a church despite his parents having done so and despite the pervasive religious fervor of the second great awakening. He rejected common vices, such as gambling, alcohol, and tobacco. This independence of thought and strength of principle are what later enabled Lincoln to endure the intense criticism and uncertainty inherent in his decision to go to war to preserve the union and, ultimately, eradicate slavery.

As a teenager, Lincoln learned the value of ingenuity. To earn money, he had taken a job cutting wood for the steamboats on the Ohio River. On the side, and probably for his own amusement, he built his own flat-bottomed boat. Soon, he was approached by two men who asked that he row them from the shore to the steamboat in the river. For his troubles, Lincoln earned a dollar—a considerable amount of money in those days. Years later, Lincoln recalled that it "was the most important incident in my life. I could scarcely credit that I, a poor boy, had earned a dollar in less than a day. The world seemed wider and fairer before me."[19]

Lincoln was not a naturally brilliant man for whom learning came easy. Rather, as Horace Greeley, editor of the *New York Tribune*, described, Lincoln's mind worked "not quickly nor brilliantly, but exhaustively."[20] With native intelligence, Lincoln educated himself through toil, tears, and sweat. As such, he serves as an example not of some unreachable ideal but rather of what is possible in America through hard work, determination, and strength of character.

Lincoln's early years were training for the heroic leader that would later emerge. The qualities ingrained in Lincoln during his formative years would manifest themselves throughout his lifetime and would be the building blocks upon which Lincoln, the hero, was formed.

LINCOLN AS A LAWYER:
THE FOUNDATION OF A HERO

I t was not an accident that Lincoln became a hero or a mythic legend. His career served as an opportunity to sow the seeds of leadership that he collected through his observation and study of others during his childhood. Before he was president of the United States, Abraham Lincoln was a lawyer, and before he was a lawyer, he was a politician. The combination of these professions—which he practiced simultaneously—helped further shape Lincoln into the ultimate lawyer-statesman who, as the nation's sixteenth president, would lead the nation through civil war, save the Union from disintegration, and eliminate slavery in America.

Heroes, like great lawyers, need the ability to stay the course even when they stand alone, as Lincoln so often did. Attorneys must exercise scholarship and common sense when standing up for their clients. They have a duty and, in fact, a professional obligation to clearly articulate their arguments, which ultimately lead to the decisions that help shape and define how people in communities live, how they interact with one another, and how they should conduct themselves in their transactions and in their daily lives.

Lincoln practiced law for twenty-four years, from 1837 until his presidency began in 1861. He embodied what makes a great lawyer. During his quarter-century career as a lawyer, Lincoln honed his political skills. He learned the art of debate, the weight of words, and the skill of negotiating. As a result, he was sharper than John C. Calhoun in understanding the foundation of democratic political theory; he could more than hold his own in the debates with Stephen A. Douglas, the political "Little Giant," who would "blow out the moral lights around us" with the extension of slavery in the territories, and he was more than a match for the aging Chief Justice of the U.S. Supreme Court Roger B. Taney—majority author of the infamous *Dred Scott* decision with its derisive comment that the black man "had no rights which the white man was bound to respect."[1]

No one knows precisely when Lincoln first decided to become a lawyer. His legal education was largely the product of self-study and all the years he spent as a pioneer child reading and absorbing anything he could get his hands on. After five years living on Knob Creek, Lincoln's family moved to Indiana, and legend has it that he read his first law book, *The Revised Laws of Indiana*, while still a youth living in that state. Ironically, Lincoln's first exposure to the law may have been as a criminal defendant, when he was charged in Kentucky with operating a ferryboat without a license. The charges arose from transporting passengers on his flatboat from the shore to awaiting passenger ferries on the Ohio River. Ultimately, the magistrate presiding over the case dismissed the charges against him after consulting the Kentucky statute and determining that Lincoln's boat was not a ferryboat under the law.[2] The experience illustrated for Lincoln the liberating power from knowledge of the law and likely influenced his later decision to study law. At the age of twenty-one, his family relocated to Illinois, where his training took root. Rather than roaming the woods, he began spending time in courthouses at Rockport and Booneville, watching cases such as quarrels over missing livestock, suits for slander in which women defended themselves against charges of prostitution, disputes over land, disputes over bad debts, and disputes among neighbors. His time as an onlooker in the courtroom offered not only entertainment but also great edification. In some ways, lawyers were Lincoln's heroes, giving the prairie boy a way out of the hard labor that would otherwise have become his responsibility.

Lincoln learned the law by reading legal treatises such as Sir William Blackstone's *Commentaries on the Laws of England*, *Chitty on Pleading*, *Greenleaf on Evidence*, and *Story on Equity*. "Get the books and read,

read, read, is the main thing" he would tell a young correspondent who wanted to be a lawyer. He also gained practical legal experience by serving as a lawyer's apprentice. After submitting a certificate of good character—Illinois had no bar examination requirement at the time—Lincoln received his law license from the Illinois Supreme Court on September 9, 1836, and was formally admitted to the bar the following year.

Nevertheless, Lincoln had not set out initially to become a lawyer. He held at least nine different jobs before turning to the law. Most notable of these jobs was his stint as state representative. In fact, Lincoln ran for office at a younger age than any other lawyer who became president, and he was one of the few who ran for office *before* he became a lawyer. It was in 1832, at the age of twenty-three, that Lincoln made his first attempt to enter politics, unsuccessfully running for a seat in the Illinois General Assembly. Although defeated in this first effort, due to his lack of time to campaign for the position as he was then enlisted in the Black Hawk War, it helped him recognize the satisfaction that comes from working on political problems facing one's community. Two years later, he was elected as an Illinois state representative.

For the next twenty-four years of his life, Lincoln served as an attorney of the Illinois bar.[3] His law practice covered every part of the legal spectrum, but the bulk of his work consisted of ordinary matters commonly handled by small-town lawyers with a general practice, just as he had once observed as a spectator: "[P]roperty disputes, petty criminal cases, family arguments over money, neighbor at war with neighbor, bankruptcies, and, oddly, libel suits where local women defended themselves against charges of prostitution" were among the matters that fueled Lincoln's law practice. He argued cases as varied as the validity of a slave as consideration for a promissory note to ownership of a vagrant pig. One commentator described his practice as the "legal equivalent of a small-town doctor's [practice], treating head colds, lice, scarlet fever, and a rare case or two of venereal disease."[4]

Most of Lincoln's law practice took place while "traveling the circuit" in the Eighth Judicial Circuit of Illinois.[5] The Eighth Judicial Circuit at that time encompassed fourteen counties, about the size of Connecticut. Court was held for a week or two in each county seat, with lawyers following the presiding justice from county to county. Riding the circuit gave Lincoln the opportunity to try a variety of criminal and civil cases before the various circuit judges, but it was exhausting.[6] He spent weeks at a time away from home; the days were long, the travel was difficult, the food was bad, and the lodging was worse. Justice was dispensed hastily and informally. Lawyers met with their clients only for a short time before going to trial, and decisions were made on the spot. Nevertheless, Lincoln seemed to enjoy riding the circuit, which proved immensely important in shaping him for what he would later encounter in the presidency. For example, because Lincoln could not anticipate the facts and the legal issues the cases presented by the cases, he quickly learned to think on his feet and to respond on a moment's notice. He inevitably developed "the knack of adjusting himself quickly to changed situations. . . . [He was] confronted with a type of practice which required a legal mind quick to find expedients."[7]

"Lincoln—The Circuit Rider," color lithograph, calendar print, Chicago & Midland Railway, 1951. Reproduction of a painting by Reynolds Jones. Lincoln was first a politician and then a lawyer. The two careers were inextricably entwined. He was a successful mediator before the word was coined. Courtesy of the Frank and Virginia Williams Collection of Lincolniana.

Traveling the circuit also developed in Lincoln several other attributes that would later prove useful in national politics. Importantly, he learned how to focus his extraordinary energy while pursuing his dual legal and political careers. Because of his simultaneous careers, he developed the ability to be a masterful juggler, handling a heavy legal practice and a demanding schedule as a working legislator and emerging leader of his party. Performing these multiple tasks at the same time later would prove essential in the presidency, which requires an individual to manage multiple roles: commander in chief, chief executive, chief diplomat, party leader, legislative leader, and voice of the people. He also developed a strong sense of self-confidence during his practice as a lawyer. All of these skills added to Lincoln's greatness.

If there is one characteristic of a hero that was solidified in Lincoln through his practice of law and subsequent political career, it is his skill as a communicator. Historian Paul Johnson, commenting on Lincoln, notes, "Words, and the ability to weave them into webs which cling to the memory, are extremely important in forwarding political action. This was already true in semiliterate fifth-century B.C. Athens, as Thucydides makes clear, and in republican Rome, as Shakespeare, with his uncanny gift for getting history right, shows brilliantly in Julius Caesar."[8]

Lincoln's dual legal and political careers provided him with a unique opportunity to improve his almost instinctive inclination to search for the best way to communicate. He never ceased working to improve his writing and his ability to construct verse. As a result of his fascination with words, he developed a philosophical and almost poetic understanding of the law, politics, and life. For this reason, he had gained a great knack for speaking to a jury and putting an entire case into focus in an appealing manner. One of his colleagues once described him as "the plainest man [I] had ever heard. He was not a speaker, but a talker. He talks to jurors . . . almost as in conversation, no effort whatsoever in oratory. But his talking had a wonderful effect. Honesty, candor, fairness, everything that was convincing, was in his manner and expressions."[9] Lincoln knew that people judged cases as much by their hearts as by their heads. Fellow attorney Lawrence

Weldon wrote, "Mr. Lincoln's speeches to the jury were most effective specimens of forensic oratory. He talked the vocabulary of the people, and the jury understood every point he made and every thought he uttered. . . . He constructed short sentences of small words, and never wearied the mind with mazes of elaboration."[10]

Without his long career that required sharp faculties in the give-and-take of both the courtroom and the floor of the legislature, Lincoln would have been ill-prepared to match Douglas in their famous debates. Lincoln's performance in those classic debates helped to propel him into the presidency.

Lincoln's exhaustive approach to learning served him well as an attorney. His last law partner, William H. Herndon, admired that Lincoln "not only went to the root of the question, but dug up the root, and separated and analyzed every fiber of it."[11]

An ability to identify the central issue in a legal problem is one of the most critical skills required for a lawyer. Lincoln often success-fully outmaneuvered adversaries by conceding peripheral issues while zealously advocating for the essential ones. Fellow attorney Leonard Swett observed, "Any man who took Lincoln for a simple-minded man would very soon wake up with his back in a ditch."[12]

Not surprising, Lincoln's law practice reflected his Whig philoso-phy, which favored settlement of disputes in the interest of commu-nity order. Indeed, Lincoln believed in alternative dispute resolution before that phrase was even coined. He learned to detach himself from the issues and, like every good negotiator, seek out a middle ground between adversaries. One of his law clerks once stated that he often overheard Lincoln telling prospective clients, "You have no case; better settle."[13] In fact, about 33 percent of Lincoln's more than fifty-five hundred cases were dismissed, and many of these can be attributed to settlement or mediation. This attribute would later reemerge to the nation's benefit during his presidency.

As an attorney, Lincoln struck a balance between zealous advo-cacy for his clients and a good sense of professional courtesy, which translated into honesty and integrity.[14] He once declared, "I mean to put a case no stronger than the truth will allow." One of Lincoln's col-leagues, discussing Lincoln's courtroom demeanor, stated, "[Lincoln] never misstated evidence, but stated clearly and fairly and squarely his opponent's case."[15] Indeed, as author Brian Dirck notes in *Lincoln the Lawyer*, "no one seems to have ever accused [Lincoln] of being an unethical attorney."[16] In one instance, after meeting with a potential client, Lincoln told the man, "Yes, there is no reasonable doubt but that I can gain your case for you; I can set a whole neighborhood at loggerheads; I can distress a widowed mother and her six fatherless children, and thereby get for you $600 which you seem to have a legal claim to; but which rightfully belongs, it appears to me, as much to the woman and her children as it does to you. You must remember some things that are legally right are not morally right. I shall not take your case—but I will give you a little advice for which I charge nothing. You seem to be a sprightly, energetic man, I would advise you to try your hand at making $600 in some other way."[17]

On another occasion, Lincoln and attorney Swett were appointed to defend a man indicted for murder. When Lincoln and Swett consulted the defendant, Lincoln became convinced that the defendant was guilty. Although he tried to convince Swett that the only way to save the defendant was to advise him to plead guilty and appeal to the court for leniency, Swett would not agree to Lincoln's suggestion, so the case went to trial. Lincoln did not participate during the trial. In fact, he took no part in it other than to make an occasional suggestion to Swett during the examination of witnesses. Ultimately, the defendant was acquitted on technical grounds. When the jury rendered its verdict, Lincoln reached over Swett's shoulder, with the fifty dollars he had received from the defendant, saying, "Here, Swett, take this money. It is yours. You earned it, not I."[18]

Lincoln's integrity is best illustrated by a story he told when explaining what influenced him in choosing the law as his profession. He explained that a widow had lost her cow when it was killed by a railroad train. She had hired him to represent her and sue the company for damages. Before bringing suit, the railroad company approached Lincoln with the proposition that if he would throw over the widow, the company would remunerate him handsomely and give him legal work connected with the railroad. Lincoln refused. Instead, not only did Lincoln take her case but he also won it for her.[19]

During another case, during a trial in Metamora, Woodford County, Illinois, Lincoln realized that the case was proceeding poorly for his client, Mrs. Goings, who was charged with murdering her abusive husband. Lincoln called a recess so that he could confer with his client and led her from the courtroom. When court reconvened, and Mrs. Goings could not be found, Lincoln was accused of advising her to flee, a charge he vehemently denied. He explained, however, that Mrs. Goings had asked him where she could get a drink of water, and he had pointed out that Tennessee had darn good water. She was never again seen in Illinois. As it turned out, the charge against Mrs. Goings was dismissed nearly a year later on the state attorney's motion.[20] While by today's standards, Lincoln's tactic would not be tolerated and, in fact, would violate the ethical standards that govern lawyers, during Lincoln's day, there was no similar prohibition. Lawyers were expected to do all that they could to assist their clients. In this sense, Lincoln's creative strategy with respect to Mrs. Goings is heroic, at least by the standards of Lincoln's day.

As a lawyer, Lincoln also emphasized the need for civility, a quality that both the bench and bar must exercise in their daily interactions with one another. In referring to lawyers who swindle their clients, he was unyielding: "I never want the reputation enjoyed by those shining lights of the profession *Catch'em & Cheat'em.*"[21] His enthusiasm in the representation of clients' interests was tempered by knowledge that there were boundaries, both professional and moral, to his behavior. He believed in civility not only toward his clients but also toward fellow attorneys. As a colleague of his once said, "[Lincoln] would not do anything mean, or which savored of sharp practice, or which required absolute sophistry or chicanery to succeed."[22]

Not only was Lincoln a great lawyer but he was also an excellent trial attorney. He consistently demonstrated precise skill in interviewing to collect data and in his effective cross-examination of witnesses. Lincoln also knew how to strike the ideal balance for courtroom demeanor and avoid overly aggressive behavior. Lincoln possessed what one observer called "courtroom finesse to an extraordinary degree."[23] He had a reputation as a tenacious litigator, one who knew how to employ a technicality or pitch an argument to get what was needed. People underestimated him at their peril.

Lincoln's ability as a mediator was mostly demonstrated in the slander cases he handled, many of which contained accusations against women of adultery or fornication.[24] An illustration of one of Lincoln's typical slander cases involved a woman by the name of Eliza Cabot, who complained that Francis Regnier wrongly accused her of fornication. Lincoln, who represented Cabot, ultimately secured a verdict of $1,600 for her. In these matters, Lincoln was involved heavily in maintaining community reputations and relationships; he played the role of mediator in order to restore peace to the neighborhood and keep the charges out of the courtroom.[25] He was able to resolve many cases by repairing the damage to the plaintiffs' reputations. In several cases, Lincoln had the defendant attest to the good reputation of the slandered plaintiff, which would usually settle the case out of court. Lincoln's settlement strategy demonstrated his sensitivity to what was actually at stake in these cases. Fellow lawyer James C. Conkling observed, "Like most lawyers in small communities, [Lincoln] was keenly aware that the community orientation of those disputes favored mediation and compromise, and he thus tried to serve as mediator or peace maker."[26]

Commenting on the power of colonial lawyers at the time of the American Revolution, Edmund Burke declared, "This study [of law] renders men acute, inquisitive, dexterous, prompt in attack, ready in defense, full of resources. No other profession is more closely connected with actual life than the law. It concerns the highest of all temporal interests of man—property, reputation, the peace of all families, the arbitrations and peace of nations, liberty, life even, and the very foundations of society"[27] It is from this mold that Lincoln was formed, and, as his political career would later demonstrate, Lincoln perfected that mold, using all of the skills he developed as a lawyer to save the nation and unite it.

As an attorney, Lincoln showed unusual political courage when he was called upon to defend progress in 1857. At this time, the future of transportation innovation was at stake—old riverboat technology was pitted against new railroad-bridge technology.[28] The Rock

Island Railroad Company had hired Lincoln as lead counsel to defend it in the case of *Hurd v. Rock Island Railroad Company*, where the river boat *Effie Afton*, heading south on the Mississippi River, had smacked into an abutment of the railroad bridge that crossed the river, and the boat was set afire.[29] The case, tried before the U.S. circuit court in Chicago, rested on a central, key point: either the steamboat's crew or the Rock Island Bridge Company was to blame for the accident. Ultimately, Lincoln won the case by having a hung jury—the case was never retried.[30] This win effectively advanced the cause of commerce in the United States, with both railroad and river transportation, ensuring that both would become the country's prevailing mode of transportation.

During his time as an attorney, Lincoln developed a close relationship with Judge David Davis.[31] It was common then for circuit judges to designate attorneys to take their seats on the bench if they were called away. Judge Davis held Lincoln in such high regard that he chose him to take his place whenever he could not attend to his judicial labors. William H. Somers, a clerk of the Champaign circuit court, stated that he "[didn't] remember seeing [Judge Davis] extend to any other Attorney, of twenty or more in attendance" the privilege of assuming the judge's seat on the bench. Although court records do not reveal when an attorney sat in place of a judge, one can determine when Lincoln heard a case based upon an examination of the different handwriting styles entered in the judges' dockets. A thorough assessment of the judges' dockets discloses that Lincoln sat for almost three hundred cases in Judge Davis's stead.[32] Having successfully heard approximately three hundred cases as judge, it is quite clear that not only could Lincoln make a good judge but that he was, indeed, a good judge.

Lincoln sought to ensure that the people would have confidence and respect for the institution trusted to balance the scales of justice. Certainly, Lincoln's honesty and integrity permeated the courtroom when Lincoln filled in for Judge Davis. While sitting as a judge, he heard two motions Herndon argued. In one case, Lincoln decided a motion against his own client; in another, he was stern and ordered his clients "to answer by the 1st of [February] next." While other judges have been chastised for presiding over such cases, to Lincoln's credit, his colleagues had confidence in his veracity and fairness on the bench. Even Herndon's adversary did not object when Lincoln sat in place of Judge Davis on the bench. Instead, his opponent, without protest, argued the motion before Lincoln.[33] Not only do these illustrations demonstrate that Lincoln had the ability to sit as a fair and impartial judge but they also show that Lincoln could maintain such neutrality even when faced with a motion by his own law partner on behalf of his own client. The words of the late Frank M. Johnson, U.S. district and circuit judge, epitomize Lincoln as a judge: "The basic concept that a good judge has to have is to do what's right, regardless of who the litigants are, regardless of how technical, or regardless of how emotional the issues that are presented are. If you are not willing to do what's right, then you need to get you another job. So I never did think that I was entitled to any great credit for doing it, because that was my obligation. That's what I signed on to do."[34]

Lincoln embodied the qualities that make up a great judge. Great judges may speak more clearly than an act of a legislature because they are single individuals. They speak more distinctly than most judges because they have more to teach, and they speak with force and power. Lincoln had these qualities in abundance. Above all, he knew that results mattered. He was not afraid to push the envelope. He knew that he had to have courage, remain steadfast, and stand up for his beliefs. Surely, Lincoln would have been a full-time judge but for his first love—politics.

Lincoln biographers have often concluded that his legal practice ended on the day he last visited his law office. Yet, nothing could be further from the truth. It would be more accurate to say that it was just the beginning; he would then have to apply it to the highest use of all since his admission to the bar in 1837. After twenty-four years of law practice, Lincoln would serve as his own lawyer in the Executive Mansion. He continually confronted novel legal issues with a verve lacking in previous presidents.

CHAPTER THREE

LINCOLN'S INTRODUCTION TO POLITICS

S uccess does not always come easy for all heroes, but the failures
that many incur have often only made them stronger and more
determined. Undeterred by his loss at the age of twenty-three in his
bid for a seat as a representative in the Illinois General Assembly,
he exemplified the same persistence with which he approached his
studies when he campaigned again two years later and won election
as a representative to the Illinois House of Representatives.

Lincoln learned a great deal about politics during his eventual
four terms in the state house and one term in the U.S. House of
Representatives. This experience was invaluable in preparing for his
subsequent senatorial campaign against Stephen A. Douglas in 1858
and his successful bid for president two years later.

Among the most important lessons that Lincoln drew from his
early political career were an extraordinary sense of timing and an
ability to listen to others. He learned to discern when to seize the
initiative and when to bide his time. His sense of political timing
served him well later during the Civil War, when he decided to wait
for a Union victory before delivering his controversial Emancipation
Proclamation. Such a victory—albeit a costly one—occurred at the
Battle of Antietam. Five days later, on January 1, 1863, Lincoln issued the preliminary Emancipation Proclamation promising to free
all slaves in Southern states or parts of states not yet under Union
control, so as not to alienate the Border States, which were critical
to the Union war effort.

Lincoln's political success would not have been possible, however, without his exceptional oratorical skills, which owed to his well-earned command of the English language and profound sense of history and philosophy. It also came from his study of *The Columbian Orator*, which exposed him to the classical works of rhetorical giants such as Socrates and Cicero, and an essay on effective public speaking. Lincoln's speeches, which are among the finest pieces of oration, were carefully crafted, reflecting the same thoroughness with which he approached learning.

For instance, Lincoln spoke about the issue of equality with passion and conviction. Take this letter to a friend: "When we were the political slaves of King George, and wanted to be free, we called the maxim that 'all men are created equal' a self-evident truth, but now when we have grown fat, and have lost all dread of being slaves ourselves, we have become so greedy to be *masters* that we call the same maxim 'a self-evident lie.'"[1]

Perhaps the most convincing example of Lincoln's rhetorical skill is the Gettysburg Address. Lasting a mere two minutes and spanning less than three hundred words, his address to an audience at the dedication of the cemetery at Gettysburg is the most famous speech delivered by any American president. His eloquent tribute to the fallen soldiers captured the sacred spot: "[W]e can not dedicate—we can not consecrate—we can not hallow—this ground. The brave men, living and dead, who struggled here, have consecrated it, far above our poor power to add or detract."[2]

When Lincoln gave his address amid the graves that lie in Gettysburg row upon row, he did not believe that his words would enter the fabric of American democracy for eternity, but his words struck a chord in America's collective heart. A New England reporter—one of the first to comment on the Gettysburg Address—lauded Lincoln's eloquent brevity: "It is often said that the hardest thing in the world to do is to make a five minutes' speech. But could the most elaborate and studied oration be more beautiful, more touching, more inspiring, than those few thrilling words of the President?"[3]

Apart from demonstrating his exceptional oratory skills, the Gettysburg address also reflected his strong convictions about the country and its ability to thrive and prosper.[4] In fact, if there was one trait that Lincoln carried with him from the practice of law into the practice of politics, it was his strong conviction. In a nation that had made upward mobility possible for him, he favored a transformed Constitution in tune with the natural-rights jurisprudence of the Declaration of Independence so that, at least theoretically, all men (and women), regardless of race, were equal. It was perhaps his deep understanding of people, which he developed through the practice of law, that solidified this belief in him.

Lincoln opposed slavery in public even when taking that position was politically risky. After all, he lost the U.S. Senate seat he contested with Douglas in 1858. Republican Lincoln and Democrat Douglas were engaged in a battle to win not just an Illinois seat in the United States Senate but control of the state legislature for their respective parties. Indeed, when Douglas learned his fate was to spar with Lincoln for the Senate seat, he recognized that he would be up against a worthy opponent. "I shall have my hands full," he told a reporter. "He is as honest as he is shrewd; and if I beat him, my victory will be hardly won."[5] Although Douglas was the incumbent and one of the country's most formidable politicians, Lincoln managed to stand out during these debates, not only as an impressive opponent of Douglas but also as a vigorous spokesman of the new Republican party.

In accepting his nomination for a seat on the U.S. Senate, Lincoln directly, in one of his greatest (and most controversial) speeches, challenged Douglas and the Democratic system of beliefs. In his house-divided speech, Lincoln proclaimed, "A house divided against itself cannot stand. I believe this government cannot endure permanently half *slave* and half *free*."[6] Although Lincoln made clear that he did not expect the house to fall or the Union to dissolve, he did expect that it would cease to be divided. He delivered this speech in June 1858. Two months later, the debates began.

Rather than make speeches independent of one another, Lincoln suggested, in a July 24, 1858, letter, an opportunity in which the two candidates could appear together, tackle the same issues, and address the same audiences. Douglas agreed to the joint appearances but only after Lincoln had followed him around Illinois, watching Douglas from the audience and inviting the audience by broadside or word of mouth to attend his rejoinder the next day. Douglas's acceptance of the joint-appearance proposal was a strategic mistake on his part for these debates leveled the playing field for the candidates and put Lincoln on a virtual par with the incumbent. They also presented a forum for Lincoln to question Douglas directly, leaving him in a position where he could not avoid an answer.

Prior to the Lincoln-Douglas debates, political candidates campaigned by traveling from town to town and gathering crowds before making political speeches. Most often, the candidate delivered his speech while perched upon a sawed-off tree stump by which he set himself apart from the crowd. This practice was most prominent on the frontier, where there was a shortage of meeting houses and public halls. Reflecting its origins, this manner of speaking became known as a "stump speech."

"Lincoln—The Campaigner," color lithograph, calendar print, Chicago & Midland Railway, 1951), reproduction of a painting by Reynolds Jones. Politics was Lincoln's first love, developed early in his life. He gave his first political speech in Decatur, Illinois, when he was twenty-one years old. Courtesy of the Frank and Virginia Williams Collection of Lincolniana.

The seven, three-hour-long contests between Lincoln and Douglas reflected the traditional format of debate, with no moderator or press panel. The format was simple yet effective. One candidate spoke for one hour. Next, his opponent spoke for an hour and a half. Then the first candidate had a final half hour for rebuttal. Lincoln and Douglas alternated as the first speaker in the debates. As an incumbent, Douglas made four of the opening and closing statements; Lincoln only three.

The issue of slavery played the most dominant role in the debates. Although Lincoln was morally and politically opposed to slavery, he was careful not to pass judgment on Southern slaveholders. He assured them that it was not his intention to interfere with slavery where it already existed. Nevertheless, in lawyer-like fashion, he set forth his well-developed arguments against the spread of slavery in America.

One cannot help observing, however, that even while carefully choosing his words and his battles, Lincoln's repugnance of slavery asserted itself. As Lincoln stated in the first debate, "This *declared* indifference . . . for the spread of slavery, I can not but hate. I hate it because of the monstrous injustice of slavery itself. I hate it because it deprives our republican example of its just influence in the world—enables the enemies of free institutions, . . . to taunt us as hypocrites—causes the real friends of freedom to doubt our sincerity, and especially because it forces so many good men amongst ourselves into an open war with the very fundamental principles of civil liberty—criticizing the Declaration of Independence, and insisting that there is no right principle of action but *self-interest*."[7] Criticizing Douglas's position on slavery, Lincoln remarked during the first debate, "When [Douglas] invites any people, willing to have slavery, to establish it, he is blowing out the moral lights around us."[8]

Lincoln not only defended his positions articulately but the ever-persuasive lawyer used the debates as an opportunity to force Douglas to choose between two positions, both of which were damaging. In lawyer-like fashion, Lincoln presented questions to Douglas, knowing full well how his opponent would respond. At the second debate when Lincoln asked, "Can the people of a United States Territory, in any lawful way, against the wish of any citizen of the United

States, exclude slavery from its limits prior to the formation of a State Constitution?" the question forced Douglas to acknowledge the shortcoming in his popular sovereignty argument—the policy leaving it to the new states to decide whether slavery would exist or not.[9]

The seven formal debates between Lincoln and Douglas were only a small part of the 1858 campaign, but they attracted the greatest public interest. For three months in 1858, Lincoln and Douglas crisscrossed Illinois, traveling nearly ten thousand miles, to bring these face-to-face debates to the public. For the first time, reporters were assigned to cover the candidates through the entire lengthy campaign season.

These debates were the first in history in which the media played a significant role. Newspapers of the nineteenth century were largely party-affiliated products. Articles written about the Lincoln-Douglas debates are laden with the author's opinions and often do not even relate to the issues presented by the candidates. Despite the reporters' biases, they provided a lens through which the public could closely follow the candidates. It was through the newspapers that the nation learned about Lincoln, his beliefs, and his policies.

Reporters noted how sharply the two candidates contrasted in appearance and style. Douglas was so short that he stood equal to Lincoln's shoulders, whereas Lincoln was exceptionally tall and painfully thin. Douglas used graceful gestures and was charming, whereas Lincoln moved awkwardly. Their speaking styles were quite different as well. Douglas was more apt to use rhetoric, whereas Lincoln spent most of his time and energy on reasoning.

Recognizing that the partisan nature of the press could lead to inaccuracies, Lincoln clipped his speeches from newspapers sympathetic to the Republican Party and the speeches of Douglas from the Democratic press. Lincoln occasionally made notes in the margins when he felt the reporting required changes or comment. In fact, Lincoln had his own version of the debates published and distributed nationally to promote his political career. His version of the debates became something like a bestseller, selling more than thirty thousand copies.[10] Today, his original scrapbook of the debates with his own emendations to the debates remains on display in the

Library of Congress. Perhaps motivated by the fact that he might run for president, as well as his own desire to have an accurate record of his arguments, Lincoln sought to have these debates made available to the public, as they directly exhibited his views on the issue of the day—slavery.

The Lincoln-Douglas debates have proved momentous, yet it is important to remember that Lincoln had lost the Senate race to Douglas, though he came close to toppling the "Little Giant," whom almost everyone thought was unbeatable.

But all was not lost. Though he did not become a U.S. Senator, he became the face of the new Republican party. Relatively unknown before the Lincoln-Douglas debates, the debates turned him into a national figure and propelled him to the presidency. By the end of the debates, Lincoln had gained notoriety and respect. The widespread media coverage raised Lincoln's national profile. In the words he used during his first debate with Douglas, "public sentiment is everything. With public sentiment, nothing can fail; without it nothing can succeed."[11]

Lincoln's eloquent oratory skills thrust him into the limelight, where he garnered positive public sentiment in abundance. It was perhaps this skill that made America warm to the young politician and provided a solid foundation for his later elevation as a hero.

CHAPTER FOUR

FINDING A HERO IN
A MILITARY NEOPHYTE

S ome say that great leaders are born, not made. They believe that there are individuals who are destined to rise to leadership when needed. If this is true, there is virtually no explanation for Abraham Lincoln, a simple prairie boy from Middle-of-Nowhere, USA, and his tremendous leadership through the Civil War. The skills Lincoln honed as a lawyer and statesman are, at least in part, what came to make him a heroic military leader.

When he took his oath as the sixteenth President of the United States on March 4, 1861, Lincoln became commander in chief of a deeply divided nation. This would be an arduous role for any president, let alone one who had less experience in public office than any previous president, with the exception of Zachary Taylor and William Henry Harrison.

Some heroes become legends because of their fighting—like those in Homer's *Iliad*—but fighting has not brought Lincoln acclaim. Lincoln lacked serious military experience, especially in contrast to his adversary Jefferson Davis, a West Point graduate, a Mexican War colonel and hero, and a former Secretary of State. Indeed, Lincoln often joked about his brief army career: three months' service with several rag-tag militia companies in the Black Hawk War. His first exposure to war came in 1832, when he volunteered for the Black Hawk War and served for thirty days as the elected captain of his local militia company and sixty more as a private. Lincoln, however, did not see combat, except, as he later joked, in battling pesky mosquitoes.[1]

As a captain in the war, Lincoln inspired more humor than gallantry as a leader, but that was part of his charm. Once, when marching his company toward a narrow gate, he forgot the proper command to form his troops into a single line so they could advance. "Halt!" Lincoln finally shouted. "This company is dismissed for two minutes, when it will form again on the other side of the gate."[2] Lincoln's actions were not classically military, but they were ingenious and wise. After all, a hero is one who can adapt when the situation is not going quite the way he or she wants or hopes.

In truth, Lincoln's service in the Black Hawk War should not be underestimated. His election as captain led him to reflect almost thirty years later that no subsequent success of his life gave him as much satisfaction as leading the militiamen as their elected captain. The election by his peers was a first in his life, no doubt boosting his self-esteem. The men of his Black Hawk War company testified that their captain had shown himself "a kind hearted & noble man who did his duty well without fear[,] gold, favor or Affection. He had a somewhat good Eye for Military affairs, as said by Competent judges." Even back then, a New Salem friend marveled, "His heart & head were large & Comprehensive enough to Command a Company—regiment or other Core [sic] of men under any Circumstances."[3] Lincoln was a civilian by habit, experience, and vision. Yet, his background served him well when he led the citizen soldiers who fought the Civil War.

One of the most important lessons for young Lincoln was that exuberant young men could not make the transition from civilians to soldiers overnight and would never fully transform themselves into full-time military men. He also learned that raw recruits came from a democratic culture with a high disregard for authority. Many of these civilian soldiers in the end simply could not, and would not, recognize the right of the military to keep them in service longer than they wished to stay. Such an attitude owed little or nothing to cowardice, laziness, and lack of patriotism but had a great deal to do with a cultural instinct for independence. Lincoln shared their privations, especially hunger: the military supply system worked imperfectly at best, and the soldiers often went without rations. When his men went hungry, so did he, on one occasion passing two days without food. Instinctively, he understood that good humor, patience, a willingness to share equally in the hardships of the privates, and an absence of self-importance were the primary basis to provide leadership and to bind the men to him.[4] Fortunately, these characteristics were already a part of his midwestern nature. Lincoln was heroic not for his actions on the battlefield but for the manner in which he oversaw the proper functions of the military. Lincoln was acutely aware that many of the nation's soldiers were mere boys called to manhood too soon. So potent was his sense of responsibility for the lives of these young men that Lincoln walked among them daily, talking and listening to them as a father would. Indeed, many soldiers would come to call him Father Abraham.[5]

Historian William C. Davis in *Lincoln's Men: How President Lincoln Became Father to an Army and a Nation* reinforces the idea that the most important Lincoln lesson was that young men, as enthusiastic or patriotic as they may be, could not be turned from peaceful civilians into soldiers overnight.[6] This helped him relate to the soldiers serving under him in the Civil War, as he knew firsthand what it was like to endure delays in rations, supplies, and pay—to have to sleep on the cold ground and put up with the indefinite waiting. He knew that it took training, discipline, belief in a chain of command, loyalty, and a commitment to success.[7]

With this minimalist background, Lincoln inherited the presidency and its powers as commander in chief. By his inauguration on March 4, 1861, seven states had already seceded from the Union, and six had joined together in the newly formed Confederate States of America. The nation was on the brink of civil war, and Lincoln had resolved to prevent it from falling further apart.

In the ten weeks between the outbreak at Fort Sumter and the convening of Congress in special session on July 4, 1861, Lincoln acted. He added twenty-three thousand men to the regular army and eighteen thousand to the navy. He called forty thousand volunteers for three years' service and summoned the state militias into a ninety-day volunteer force. He paid $2 million dollars from the Treasury's unappropriated funds for purposes Congress unauthorized and closed the post office to "treasonable correspondence." He imposed a blockade on Southern ports, suspended the writ of habeas corpus in certain parts of the country, and caused the arrest and military detention of persons "who were represented to him" as engaging in or contemplating "treasonable practices."[8] He later instituted a militia draft when voluntary recruiting broke down and extended the suspension of the *habeas corpus* privilege nationwide for persons "guilty of any disloyal practice."[9]

The war was a difficult mission from the start. Initially, many Union commanders were incompetent. Their military plans frequently miscarried, so changes in strategy had to be swiftly devised and implemented. Like many heroes, Lincoln understood the need to learn from his mistakes and that a sin of omission was far worse than a sin of commission. Acutely aware of his own lack of military experience, Lincoln quickly recognized the need to educate himself when he became commander in chief. The need was exacerbated by: (1) the severity of the war, which began almost immediately after he took office; (2) a shortage of capable and decisive generals upon whom he could rely; and (3) the lack of precedent delineating the war powers of the commander in chief. As a strong and active individual, Lincoln was forced to take part in the conduct of the war. And he did so from the outset.

In contrast, Lincoln's chief adversary, Jefferson Davis, who was far more experienced in the art of war, was trapped by his own background. Davis was strident, locked in the past, and too full of himself to learn and grow. He, unlike Lincoln, micromanaged all. Once Davis made up his mind about a man or an issue, he would not change and had none of Lincoln's political skills in dealing with men—even military men. He also was guilty of favoritism with his appointments. In contrast, Lincoln was a master of making use of men—even those he did not like—if it would help the war. He could, unlike Davis, subordinate his feelings to the greater need. Lincoln, who had far less experience than Davis, could learn and grow and to that end set about mastering military strategy. His private secretary

John Hay recalled hearing Lincoln pace back and force at night in his bedroom at the White House while studying books on military strategy or poring over reports from the battlefield.[10] This is the loneliness of command.

His first major problem arose in regard to Union forts in the South. Should they be surrendered or held? If held, should men and supplies be sent to relieve and replenish the troops? Lincoln sent a relief expedition to Fort Sumter in Charleston Harbor after a muddled period of preparation in which he failed to read orders others had prepared but that he had signed, confused the names of the warships *Powhatan* and *Pocahontas* so that the relief expedition sailed without the *Powhatan*. Lincoln never again signed an order without examining it. Jefferson Davis ordered General P. G. T. Beauregard to open fire. As Lincoln said in his second inaugural address, "And the war came."[11]

Soon, Lincoln took an active role in planning and overseeing the military operations of the Civil War, largely due to the incompetency of many of his early generals but also largely due to his own growing knowledge of military affairs. Because of his expanding political education, Lincoln also understood the political dimensions of military strategy. Despite the criticism levied at him for not appointing the most militarily qualified wartime generals, he actually displayed great strategic vision in making these selections. Each so-called political general represented an important ethnic, regional, or political constituency whose support was critical to the war effort. Historian T. Harry Williams got it right when he asserted that Lincoln became not only a better military strategist than any of his generals—perhaps save General Ulysses S. Grant—but also that he was the greatest wartime president.[12] Not bad for a man whose only military experience was a three-month battle against mosquitoes.

When necessary, Lincoln did not hesitate to disregard his professional military advisers. Both General Winfield Scott, who headed the army, and General Irwin McDowell, the field commander, advised against fighting the first battle of Manassas on the ground that more time was required for disciplining and drilling the troops. The public, however, clamored for action, and Lincoln, always in tune to political necessity, overruled the generals. The battle was fought—with disastrous result. Undaunted, the following night, Lincoln prepared a detailed plan of strategy.

When Lincoln made mistakes as a war leader, he learned from them. He grew as a strategist; he asked questions; he read; he probed—anything within his power to win and shorten the war. He did not always attempt to force his tentative strategy on others. Often he submitted to the advice of his generals. Occasionally, they disregarded his wishes if not his direct orders.

As the war developed, Lincoln became even more concerned with questions of strategy. He was greatly troubled by his inability to motivate General George B. McClellan into action. In December 1861, Lincoln presented an elaborate memorandum to McClellan, asking technical questions and making suggestions about the advance on Richmond up the peninsula. The overconfident McClellan returned it with penciled replies and a note rejecting the suggestions.

On January 27, 1862, Lincoln issued his General War Order No. 1, in which he fixed February 22, Washington's birthday, as "the day for a general movement of the land and naval forces of the United States against the insurgent forces." The Army of the Potomac and others, as well as certain naval forces, were ordered to "be ready for a movement on that day." Four days later, Lincoln supplemented this with President's Special War Order No. 1, commanding the Army of the Potomac, after providing for the defense of Washington, to move on February 22 to seize Manassas Junction. This was followed on February 3 by a note to McClellan insisting upon Lincoln's own plan for an attack on the Confederate army near Washington rather than an expedition by water against Richmond.[13] Nevertheless, his plans, suggestions, and orders were ineffective in motivating McClellan or his army into action.

By this time, Lincoln had come to have serious misgivings about the judgments of professional soldiers. In his usual mild-tempered style, Lincoln had bent over backwards for McClellan, giving him all possible chances to redeem himself, but the popular general never did redeem himself. When McClellan took the field in spring 1862, Lincoln relieved him as general in chief on the grounds that one man could not direct an army engaged in active operations and at the same time plan moves for other armies. Lincoln told many people why he removed McClellan. The exasperated president concluded that McClellan had a case of the "SLOWS." "He is an admirable engineer," Lincoln was supposed to have said of McClellan, "but he seems to have a special talent for a stationary engine."[14]

Lincoln's treatment of McClellan and, in particular, his initiative in firing a popular general at a time when he himself was waning in popularity due to the state of the war set the stage for President Harry S. Truman's firing of General Douglas MacArthur, who during the Korean War similarly defied a president's directives. In fact, upon studying Lincoln's treatment of McClellan, Truman came to recognize that Lincoln is today one of the most honored presidents and McClellan one of the least valued military generals.[15] With that recognition and Lincoln's heroic actions as precedent, Truman relieved MacArthur.

Lincoln did not appoint another officer to the position until July 1862. In the interim, Lincoln acted as his own general in chief. The ever serious commander in chief went so far as to educate himself even further on military strategy. The autodidact read Henry W. Halleck's translation of the Swiss military theorist Antoine-Henri Jomini's *Life of Napoleon* and held long conversations with officers on the art of war.[16] Although inclined at first to defer to his generals' opinions, he now felt a growing confidence in his own powers to decide military questions and was perhaps a little too ready to impose his opinions on his generals.

When Stonewall Jackson made one of his forays into the Shenandoah Valley, Lincoln gave specific orders to Generals McDowell, Don Carlos Buell, and John Frémont to surround and capture Jackson and his army. Frémont disobeyed two of the president's orders, resting his men one day when they were ordered to march and again taking a different route from the one Lincoln had selected. Even if the orders had been obeyed, the capture of Jackson's army would not have been a simple task. After this experience, Lincoln did not again attempt to direct the field movements of armies a long distance from the Executive Mansion.

Several presidents have faced major crises either in bringing field generals to engage in battle or in keeping them within bounds, not simply on the battlefield but within the framework of constitutional government. General McClellan, the most lagging of field generals, was a great trial to Abraham Lincoln in both spheres. Bold in his strategic conceptions, McClellan nevertheless dreaded the actual execution of his plans. A repetitive pattern for him was to demand more reinforcements after overestimating the enemy's strength and depreciating his own. He was a wonderfully imaginative procrastinator. If catching Robert E. Lee at a disadvantage, McClellan almost invariably failed to exploit it. He must wait, McClellan would report to his impatient superiors in Washington, until the Potomac rose to be sure that Lee would not recross it; he must finish drilling new recruits, reorganize his forces, and procure more shoes, uniforms, blankets, and camp equipment.

McClellan compensated for battlefield inaction by spending his battle-idle time pouring irrepressible arrogance into his letters, including one to Lincoln on July 7, 1862, pointing out that it was high time the government established a civil and military policy to cover the full canvass of the nation's troubles and "generously" informed the president what precisely that policy should be.[17] McClellan's behavior became critical after his failure to follow up his victory at Antietam by pursuing Lee's fleeing army. Lincoln worked mightily, as his secretary John Nicolay put it, at "poking sharp sticks into little Mac's ribs."[18] When the general included among his ingenious excuses that a pandemic had afflicted the horses with sore mouths and weary backs, Lincoln was goaded into a sharp reply. "I have just read your despatch about sore tongued and fatiegued [sic] horses," he telegraphed. "Will you pardon me for asking what the horses of your Army have done since the battle of Antietam that fatigue anything?"[19]

Lincoln and his administration were now at a critical juncture. Winter was approaching and would assure that, with the exception of Antietam, the long record of Eastern defeat and stalemate would remain intact. Congress, restive with this state of affairs, was soon to convene. Governors were nervous, the cabinet was divided, and both the extreme war and peace men were thundering against the president.

Nor was Lincoln unmindful of McClellan's personal softness toward the South and the presence on his staff of some who advocated a waiting game to prolong the war until both sides were exhausted and the Union might be preserved with slavery intact. Should he replace McClellan? Alternative generals were a sorrowfully undistinguished lot, many already scarred with failure, and others abysmally inexperienced.

After serious deliberation, Lincoln relieved McClellan on November 5, 1862, and appointed General Ambrose E. Burnside in his place. Upon reading the president's order, McClellan explained, "Alas for my poor country."[20] Some among his officers even urged him to disobey the presidential order. McClellan later wrote that he could easily have marched his troops into Washington and taken possession of the government. If so, it would have been the first successful forward movement of the war. Instead, McClellan turned over the command of his 120,000 men in an elaborate ceremony. But this was by no means the last encounter between McClellan and Lincoln. In 1864, two years after his removal, McClellan met Lincoln on new terrain—as the Democratic nominee for the presidency. McClellan lost *that* battle, too.

As Lincoln came to see it, a wartime president's principal role was to press his generals into action. McClellan was not the only commander who tested the president's patience. On October 16, 1863, through Chief of Staff General Halleck, Lincoln sent to George Gordon Meade a curious letter that was in effect an order to attack Lee and that concluded, "The honor will be his if he succeeds, and the blame may be mine if he fails."[21] The letter was widely publicized, and administration newspapers hailed the president as a great strategist.

Lincoln himself laid no claim to military genius and frankly admitted that his interference with his commanders was partly the result of their dilatoriness and ineptitude and partly the result of political pressure. Expediency shaped Lincoln's military thought. He came to recognize that he had to break with the old tenets of war. As capable commanders finally emerged, Lincoln interfered less and less. He became less inclined personally to direct the strategy of the various campaigns, but he became more insistent upon generals who could work out a plan of campaign and fight.

In the beginning, hundreds of commissions were issued, many to high-ranking officers, for purely political reasons—because they had powerful friends, could raise troops, or because it was desired to obtain their full support of the war. The criticism was made—not without justification—that favoritism had officered the army with incompetence. Even when such men as Benjamin Butler and McClellan had repeatedly demonstrated their incapacity, there was long hesitation in removing them for fear of unfavorable political reaction. Butler had Radical Republican friends. McClellan had Democratic admirers. Both elements were crucial to maintain the coalition support for the war at home. After Forts Henry and Donelson and after Shiloh, in 1862, Grant had Lincoln's complete confidence, and Lincoln's reply to voluble criticism of Grant was: "I can't spare this man—he fights."[22]

Ironically, it was Lincoln, a most unlikely military man, who became America's apostle of modern war.

Lincoln never presumed to dispense completely with expert advice. Secretary of War Edwin M. Stanton convened the Army Board, consisting of the heads of the bureaus in the War Department. This was not only the general staff brought together under a chairman—the transformation of the bureau chiefs into a collective body was a forward step in command. Lincoln frequently consulted the board before arriving at an important decision.

Lincoln seemed to sense that there was something wrong in the existing arrangement. He, a civilian, was doing things that should be done by a military man. Again he decided to fill the post of general in chief. In July 1862, he named Halleck, who had been a departmental commander in the western theater, to the position.

Halleck seemed to be the ideal man for the job. Before the war, he had been known as one of the foremost American students of the art of war and a capable departmental administrator. Lincoln intended that Halleck should be a real general in chief, that he should, under the authority of the president, actually plan and direct operations.

At first, Halleck measured up to his role—but not for long. His great defect was that he disliked responsibility. He delighted to provide technical knowledge and to advise but shrank from making

Lincoln, General George M. McClellan (center), Ward Hill Lamon (seated on left), and army officers after the Battle of Antietam, October 1862, taken by Alexander Gardner. The commander in chief, with little military experience, taught himself military science. Intellectually curious and concerned for the men in the army, he visited the field eleven times—more than any other president. Courtesy of the Frank and Virginia Williams Collection of Lincolniana.

decisions. Gradually, he divested himself of his original function and deliberately assumed the part of an adviser and an informed critic.

Halleck's refusal to perform the requirements of his position forced Lincoln to act again as general in chief, but he kept Halleck as titular head of the office. The president had discovered that Halleck could do one valuable service for him—in the area of military communications. Often Lincoln and his generals had experienced serious misunderstandings because, almost literally, they spoke different languages: Lincoln the words of the lawyer-politician and the generals the jargon of the military. Halleck had lived in both the civilian and military worlds, and he could speak the language of both. Increasingly, Lincoln came to entrust the framing of his directives to Halleck.

In those years of lonely responsibility when Lincoln directed the war effort, he matured steadily in stature as a strategist. Usually he displayed greater strategic insight than most of his commanders. But he was willing, as he had been earlier, to yield the power to frame and control strategy to any general who demonstrated that he could do the job—if he could find such a general. By 1864, both he and the nation were certain they had found the man—Ulysses S. Grant. And in that year, the United States finally achieved a modern military command system to fight a modern war.

Lincoln's most important legacy as a strategist was his establishment of the modern command system: a commander in chief to lay down policy and establish overall strategy, a general in chief to frame specific battle strategy and implement plans, and a chief of staff to coordinate and relay information. Thus, Lincoln, without recognizing his long-range contribution to today's modern command system, laid its foundation in 1864. The 1864 command system embodied the brilliance of simplicity: Lincoln as commander in chief, Grant as general in chief, and Halleck as chief of staff. It contained elements that later would be studied by military leaders and students in many nations. Lincoln, without fully realizing his part, had made a large and permanent contribution to the story of command organization.

While Lincoln may never have read Carl von Clausewitz's famous treatise *On War*, his actions were a consummate expression of Clausewitz's central argument: "The political objective is the goal, war is the means of reaching it, and means can never be considered in isolation from their purpose. Therefore, it is clear that war should never be thought of as *something autonomous* but always as an instrument of policy."[23]

COURAGE TO UNDERTAKE THESE
EXTRACONSTITUTIONAL MEASURES

Chief among the characteristics that make a great leader a hero is that of courage. The circumstances that gave rise to the Civil War that Lincoln inherited as president presented opportunity after opportunity for Lincoln to demonstrate his unwavering courage. Lincoln seized upon each of these opportunities, upheld his principles, and remained steadfast even in the face of widespread criticism.

A hero is someone who can distinguish and act upon between the peripheral and the essential—between what is merely desirable and what must be done. For Lincoln, this meant all else had to be sacrificed to the overwhelming necessity of holding the Union together, behind the principles of the Declaration of Independence. As scholar James M. McPherson observes, Lincoln's focus on a singular idea aligns him with the hedgehog in British philosopher Isaiah Berlin's famous commentary on the hedgehog and the fox. Berlin describes the hedgehog as a thinker or leader who "relate[s] everything to a single central vision . . . a single, universal, organizing principle" and the fox as a leader who "pursue[s] many ends, often unrelated and even contradictory."[1] McPherson accurately describes that Lincoln is "one of the foremost hedgehogs in American history."[2] His central vision was one of America as a "nation, conceived in Liberty, and dedicated to the proposition that all men are created equal . . . shall not perish from the earth."[3] And, Lincoln would let "[n]o small matter . . . divert [him]" from the paramount goal of saving the nation.[4]

In the eighty days that elapsed between his April 1861 call for troops, marking the beginning of the Civil War, and the official convening of Congress in special session on July 4, he implemented a series of crucial acts by sheer assumption of presidential power. In April 1861, on the heels of the bombardment of Fort Sumter in Charleston Harbor by Confederate forces, Lincoln called for reinforcements to protect Washington, D.C.[5] Responding to his call for state militias, the Sixth Massachusetts Regiment arrived in Baltimore, where riots had congested the streets, and rioters attempted to prevent troops from reaching Washington.[6] The regiment from Massachusetts forged its way from one railroad station to another; twelve soldiers died, and several more were wounded.[7] By then, the Civil War was underway. The nation's capital was in jeopardy, given that it was bordered by Virginia, a secessionist state, and Maryland, whose threats to secede were widely known.[8] Newspaper headlines loudly proclaimed the horror endured by the soldiers passing through Baltimore. Giving its readers a glimpse, the *New York Times* reported, "Parties of men half frantic are roaming the streets armed with guns, pistols and muskets . . . a general state of dread prevails." In the days and weeks that followed, the city of Washington was severed from the states of the North. Troops stopped arriving, telegraph lines were slashed, and postal mail from the North reached the city only infrequently.[9]

Lincoln understood the grave danger that the war would be lost if the Confederates seized the capital or caused its complete isolation, but he was reluctant to suspend the Great Writ.[10] Finally, prompted by the urging of Secretary of State William H. Seward, Lincoln the attorney concluded that the suspension of habeas corpus could not wait.[11] Although Congress was in recess that April 1861, Lincoln, relying on the constitutional authorization that the framers had perceptively included years before, issued a proclamation suspending the writ, knowing that his duty to protect the capital and the Union required such an action.[12]

Lincoln's unilateral suspension of habeas corpus between Washington and Philadelphia was instrumental in securing communication lines to the nation's capital.[13] The effect was to enable military commanders to arrest and detain individuals indefinitely in areas where martial law was imposed.[14] Many of those detained were individuals who had attempted to halt military convoys.[15] Lincoln further understood that a declaration of martial law was necessary to divest the civil liberties of those who were disloyal and whose overt acts against the United States threatened its survival.[16]

Lincoln's actions did not go unchallenged; criticism was rampant. Despite the urgent situation, his critics bemoaned his habeas decision as an act of civil disobedience and illegal.[17] He responded to such criticism in a message to a special session of Congress on July 4, 1861:

> The provision of the Constitution that The privilege of the writ of habeas corpus, shall not be suspended unless when, in cases of rebellion or invasion, the public safety may require it," is equivalent to a provision—is a provision—that such privilege may be suspended when, in cases of rebellion, or invasion, the public safety *does* require it. It was decided that we have a case of rebellion, and that the public safety does require the qualified suspension of the privilege of the writ which was authorized to be made. Now it is insisted that Congress, and not the Executive, is vested with this power. But the Constitution itself, is silent as to which, or who, is to exercise the power; and as the provision was plainly made for a dangerous emergency, it cannot be believed that the framers of the instrument intended, that in every case, the danger should run its course, until Congress could be called together; the very assembling of which might be prevented, as was intended in this case, by the rebellion.[18]

Lincoln explained that his actions were not only justified but were required pursuant to his oath to preserve, protect, and defend the Constitution of the United States.[19] Less than one hundred days later, Congress ratified the president's actions.[20]

To Lincoln, there was no tolerable middle road. He was acutely aware that some citizens would sharply criticize him for suspending the Great Writ. The alternative, however, was far worse in his estimation. In Lincoln's judgment, nothing would be worse than allowing the nation to succumb to Confederate forces. Even some of those

"The Outbreak of the Rebellion in the United States, 1861," chromo-lithograph. Alexander Stephens, Lincoln's former colleague and now vice president of the Confederate States of America, said of him, "The Union with him in sentiment rose to the sublimity of a religious mysticism." Courtesy of the Frank and Virginia Williams Collection of Lincolniana.

who deemed Lincoln's actions unconstitutional have noted the real-world emergency that he faced. One historian comments, "Lincoln's unconstitutional acts during the Civil War show that even legality must sometimes be sacrificed for other values. We are a nation under law, but first we are a nation."[21]

Without congressional approval, Lincoln increased the size of the army and navy, expended funds for the purchase of weapons, and instituted a blockade, the latter an act of war under international law—in addition to the suspension of the writ of habeas corpus. For these actions, especially suspension of the writ, Lincoln was criticized, and is criticized still, for taking what were and are considered "extra-constitutional measures." He never denied his stretch in presidential power, but "these measures," he declared, "whether strictly legal or not, were ventured upon, under what appeared to be a popular demand, and a public necessity."[22] And in the end, his critics notwithstanding, modern scholars rank him as the nation's best leader, in part because of his broad definition of executive power.

Only a month after the proclamation, Captain Samuel Yohe, empowered by Lincoln's suspension of habeas, entered the Baltimore home of John Merryman, a discontented citizen who had spoken out vigorously against President Lincoln and had actively recruited a company of Confederate soldiers. There, Yohe arrested Merryman for various acts of treason, including his leadership of the secessionist group that conspired to destroy and ultimately did destroy railroad bridges after the Baltimore riots.[23] The government believed that Merryman's decision to form an armed group to overthrow the government was an act that went far beyond a simple expression of dissatisfaction.

Merryman's attorney sought a writ of habeas corpus, directing his petition to U.S. Supreme Court Chief Justice Roger B. Taney.[24] Merryman's lawyers suspected that Taney would entertain the petition in Washington,[25] but because he was then assigned to the Maryland circuit court, he took up the matter in Baltimore and granted the writ.[26] Despite Taney's demand to have Merryman brought before the court, George Cadwalader, the commander of the fort where Merryman was detained respectfully refused, relying on President Lincoln's suspension of habeas corpus.[27] Outraged, Taney authored *Ex parte Merryman*, opining that Congress alone—and not the president—had the power to suspend the writ of habeas corpus.[28]

The case was published in the *Federal Cases Reporter* and labeled a case from the April 1861 term of the Circuit Court for the District of Maryland, but the original opinion, in Taney's longhand, is captioned "Before the Chief Justice of the Supreme Court of the United States at Chambers."[29] Unfortunately for Chief Justice Taney, his words carry no precedential value as an "in chambers opinion." Taney recognized this but forwarded his "in chambers opinion" to President Lincoln.[30] Ironically, it was Taney who only a month before had administered the president's oath that the president now relied upon to justify his actions.[31]

If one thing is certain, it is that Chief Justice Taney's opinion did not deter Lincoln. Rather, Lincoln turned to Attorney General Edward Bates for confirmation that his decision to suspend habeas corpus was within his authority.[32] Bates responded, "I am clearly of opinion that, in a time like the present, when the very existence of the nation is assailed, by a great and dangerous insurrection, the President has the lawful discretionary power to arrest and hold in custody persons known to have criminal intercourse with the insurgents, or persons against whom there is probable cause for suspicion of such criminal complicity."[33]

Disregarding Taney's in chambers opinion, Lincoln boldly broadened the scope of the writ suspension.[34] In the draft of Lincoln's report to Congress (the only extant copy of his July 4, 1861, speech), he passionately defended his position: "The whole of the laws which were required to be faithfully executed, were being resisted, and failing of execution, in nearly one-third of the States. Must they be allowed to finally fail of execution? . . . [A]re all the laws, *but one*, to go unexecuted, and the government itself go to pieces, lest that one be violated?"[35] Lincoln ardently explained that the outbreak of the Civil War made it necessary "to call out the war power of the government and so to resist force employed for the destruction by force for its preservation" (426).

Even though the Constitution is silent with respect to which branch of government is authorized to exercise the power to suspend habeas, Lincoln's words reflected his own belief that he had exercised a power that required at least some cooperation and approval from Congress (431). Whatever confusion remained regarding the legality of Lincoln's unilateral suspension of habeas was quelled at the time, two years later when Congress, in addition to its previous ratification of August 6, 1861, enacted legislation empowering the president to suspend the writ nationwide while rebellion continued.[36]

By mid-1862, over a bloody year had passed since the onset of the Civil War. Political conflicts roiled the nation, driving both sides to fight fiercely for a cause in which each strongly believed. Despair cast a dark cloud over the country, and causalities would reach over two hundred thousand by the start of the next year.[37] Throughout the crisis, President Lincoln remained proactive, knowing that extraordinary measures were necessary to reunite the nation. On September 24, 1862, responding to the grave political and military climate, Lincoln issued another proclamation, declaring martial law and authorizing the use of military tribunals to try civilians within the United States who are believed to be "guilty of disloyal practice" or who "afford[ed] aid and comfort to Rebels."[38] This was just the beginning. The following March, Lincoln appointed Major General Ambrose E. Burnside as commanding general of the Department of the Ohio.[39] Burnside took command at his headquarters in Cincinnati, where wholesale criticism of the war was rampant. Agitated by such anti-administration speeches, Burnside responded on April 13 by issuing General Order No. 38, authorizing imposition of the death penalty for those who aided the Confederacy and who "declared sympathies for the enemy."[40]

Among those who particularly irked Burnside was former Ohio Democratic Congressman Clement L. Vallandigham, the best-known anti-war Copperhead of the Civil War and perhaps Lincoln's sharpest critic.[41] Active in politics throughout most of his life, Vallandigham was elected to the House of Representatives from Ohio in 1856, 1858, and 1860. General Burnside remembered him from several speeches that Vallandigham had given in Congress that gained considerable publicity. Vallandigham charged Lincoln with the "wicked and hazardous experiment" of calling the people to arms without counsel and authority of Congress, with violating the Constitution by declaring a blockade of Southern ports, with "contemptuously" defying the Constitution by suspending the writ of habeas corpus, and with "cooly" coming before the Congress and pleading that he was only "preserving and protecting" the Constitution and demanding and expecting the thanks of Congress and the country for his "usurpations of power."[42]

Learning that Vallandigham was scheduled to speak again at a Democratic mass meeting in Mount Vernon, Ohio, Burnside dispatched two captains in civilian clothes to listen to Vallandigham's presentation. As anticipated, Vallandigham lambasted President Lincoln, referring to him as a political tyrant and calling for his overthrow. Vallandigham proclaimed, among other things, that "the present war was a wicked, cruel, and unnecessary war, one not waged for the preservation of the Union, but for the purpose of crushing out liberty and to erect a despotism; a war for the freedom of the blacks and the enslavement of the whites."[43] With General Order No. 38 as justification and at Burnside's direction, 150 Union soldiers arrived at the Copperhead's home in Dayton, Ohio, at 2:40 A.M. on May 5, 1863.[44] When Vallandigham refused to let the soldiers in, they broke down his front door and forced their way inside.[45] After arresting him, they escorted him to Kemper Barracks, a military prison in Cincinnati.[46]

Although a U.S. citizen would ordinarily be tried for criminal offenses in the civilian court system, Vallandigham was brought before a military tribunal a day after his arrest.[47] Vallandigham, an attorney by training, represented himself before the military officers and protested that the commission had no authority to try him.[48] His protestations fell on deaf ears, however, as the case before the tribunal proceeded. The tribunal found Vallandigham guilty of violating General Order No. 38 and sentenced him to imprisonment for the duration of the war; he hired an attorney and asked for a writ of habeas corpus from the U.S. circuit court at Cincinnati, but the writ was denied.[49] He later sought from the U.S. Supreme Court a writ of certiorari, which seeks an order from a higher court directing a lower court to send it the case record so the case may be reviewed. The writ of certiorari was likewise denied, the court ruling that it was without jurisdiction to review the military tribunal's proceedings.[50]

Vallandigham's arrest, military trial, conviction, and sentence aroused excitement throughout the country. The "wiley agitator," as Lincoln later obliquely described the Ohioan, found many supporters in New York and, particularly, in heavily Democratic Albany.[51] Sentiment in Albany held that Vallandigham's arrest was arbitrary and was an effort to exert military censorship of public discourse. One newspaper reported that the arrest was an experiment the Lincoln administration conducted to test how much the public would tolerate. Many New Yorkers felt that Vallandigham's arrest posed a threat to them, too. The Albany *Atlas & Argus*, a Democratic newspaper, reported those fears: "The blow that falls upon a citizen of Ohio to-day, may be directed at a Democrat of New York to-morrow. . . . The blow, therefore, is a threat at every Democrat."[52] Four days later, the paper drove home this sentiment: "[T]he State of New York, and every citizen of the State, is equally threatened[.] We must make common cause with the citizens of other States, or we, too, are lost."[53] Democratic New Yorkers, incensed by Vallandigham's arrest, organized what the *Atlas & Argus* described as "[o]ne of the largest and most respectable meetings ever held at the Capitol"; in the protest against the case, which they believed was a "crime against the Constitution," New Yorkers arrived at the Capitol in droves, and by 8 P.M., May 16, 1863, the broad walk leading to the Capitol steps and the adjacent grounds were packed with citizens.[54]

Although unable to attend the public meeting, New York's Democratic Governor Horatio Seymour forwarded a letter that was read aloud to the spirited crowd of three thousand that filled the Capitol park.[55] Like many New Yorkers, Seymour was outraged at what he believed was a depredation of civil liberties: "The transaction involved a series of offences against our most sacred rights. It interfered with the freedom of speech; it violated our rights to be secure in our homes against unreasonable searches and seizures; it pronounced sentence without a trial, save one which was a mockery, *which insulted as well as wrong*. The perpetrators now seek to impose punishment, not for an offence against the law but for a disregard of an invalid order, put forth in an utter disregard of principles of civil liberty."[56] As the rally proceeded, fiery speeches criticized General Burnside for his action against Vallandigham. Among those who spoke were Judge Amasa J. Parker, Congressman Francis Kernan, and Judge John W. Murphy. Orator after orator expressed outrage against the allegedly arbitrary action of the administration. However, not everyone in attendance offered support for the firebrands. Several soldiers who had just returned from the battlefield displayed great dissatisfaction with the meeting's purpose, breaking chairs into pieces and hurling them into the crowd, and at one point during the disruption, it appeared as though the soldiers might seize control over the meeting, although it returned to order.[57]

Ultimately, the attendees adopted a series of resolutions and voted to send a copy to the president "with the assurance of this meeting of their hearty and earnest desire to support the Government in every Constitutional and lawful measure to suppress the existing Rebellion." The resolutions drove home the point that the attendees considered

Vallandigham's arrest and imprisonment as illegal and unconstitutional. In the Albany Democrats' opinion, "the assumption of power by a military tribunal, if successfully asserted, not only abrogates the right of the people to assemble and discuss the affairs of Government, the liberty of speech and of the press, the right of trial by jury, the law of evidence, and the privileges of *Habeas Corpus*, but it strikes a fatal blow at the supremacy of law, and the authority of the State and Federal Constitutions."[58] On May 19, 1863, Albany's former Democratic mayor, railroad entrepreneur Erastus Corning, who had been elected as president of the assemblage upon Henry S. Crandall's nomination, addressed the resolutions to Republican President Lincoln.

In the weeks after the Albany meeting, similar gatherings throughout the state of New York in Utica, Troy, and Waterloo protested what organizers insisted was the administration's infringement upon the "most sacred rights of American freemen." In Brooklyn, attendees appointed a subcommittee of the Democratic general committee to "consider the subject of the recent arbitrary arrests by the Government, and draft resolutions expressive of the sense of the Union Democratic General Committee."[59]

Those loyal to the Union and the Republican administration challenged these protests. In Albany, hundreds assembled on May 20, 1863, "to give expression to their patriotic loyalty, and to vindicate the Capital of the State of New York from the imputation of indifference to the results of the war and to the integrity of the Nation."[60] The pro-administration *Albany Evening Journal* described the assemblage of the Albany Democrats as "a meeting to justify a bad man, and to denounce those who sought to punish him. . . . The meeting was, and will be, recognized as a meeting to approve what a man, who is at heart a traitor, has said and done, rather than what its responsible managers will wish it to be deemed, viz.: a meeting to maintain the supremacy of the civil law."[61]

It was not long until Lincoln himself replied on June 12 to the Albany Democrats. In a closely reasoned document, constructed in lawyer-like fashion, and sprawling over twenty pages of handwritten sheets, Lincoln justified the action of the administration in Vallandigham's arrest, trial, imprisonment, and subsequent banishment.

He elaborated on his view that certain proceedings are constitutional "when, in cases of rebellion or Invasion, the public Safety requires them, which would not be constitutional when, in [the] absence of rebellion or invasion, the public Safety does not require them."[62] Lincoln made sure copies of his letter went not only to Corning but also to pro-Republican newspapers like the *New York Tribune*. As early as June 5, Lincoln had read the letter to his cabinet, prompting Secretary of the Navy Gideon Welles to write in his diary that the letter "has vigor and ability and with some corrections will be a strong paper."[63] In Lincoln's opinion, the framers of the Constitution were wise to include such a provision allowing for the suspension of the writ of habeas corpus, as such a suspension was necessary to prevent "sudden and extensive uprisings against the government."[64] He explained to the Albany Democrats that Vallandigham's arrest was not, as they mistakenly believed, premised on his criticism of the administration but for his avowed hostility to the Union's war efforts, his laboring to prevent the raising of troops, and his encouragement of desertions from the army.[65] Lincoln sought to assure those who harbored such mistaken beliefs that they were incorrect. Democrats in Albany had charged the Lincoln administration with arresting Vallandigham in an effort to silence him. The *Atlas & Argus* opined, "The arrest is a threat against every public man who refuses to advocate the extreme measures of the Abolition Cabinet."[66]

Vallandigham's efforts, aimed at damaging the army and leaving the Union without an adequate military force to suppress the rebellion, were intolerable to the administration and antithetical to the Union's attempt to preserve the nation. Lincoln explained that experience showed that armies cannot be maintained unless those who desert are punished by death. He believed that Vallandigham's efforts to encourage soldiers to desert the army were equally detrimental to the nation and should likewise be punished by death. With this came the most remembered passage of Lincoln's reply: "Must I shoot a simple-minded soldier boy who deserts, while I must not touch a hair of a wiley agitator who induces him to desert? . . . I think that in such a case, to silence the agitator, and save the boy, is not only constitutional, but, withal, a great mercy."[67]

Lincoln emphasized his belief that it was absolutely necessary to try insurrectionists, such as Vallandigham, before a military tribunal. In Lincoln's opinion, the civilian court system, while properly suited for trying individuals of crimes that are well defined in the law, was woefully inadequate to handle such matters as insurrection. He wrote to Corning that "a jury too frequently have at least one member, more ready to hang the panel than to hang the traitor. . . . [H]e who dissuades one man from volunteering, or induces one soldier to desert, weakens the Union cause as much as he who kills a Union soldier in battle. Yet this dissuasion, or inducement, may be so conducted as to be no defined crime of which any civil court would take cognizance."[68]

On July 3, 1863, Corning replied to the president. Showing no sign of backing down, he charged Lincoln with "pretensions to more than regal authority" and insisted that he had used "misty and cloudy forms of expression" in setting forth his pretensions. He also took issue with Lincoln's description of the group as Democrats, despite that the assemblage used this self-description in its own resolutions. They now believed that the president should have described them as American citizens. To this, Lincoln, the "wiley" politician and astute lawyer in the Executive Mansion, did not respond.

Lincoln's perceptiveness in recognizing the need to try insurrectionists by a military tribunal, rather than in the civilian court system—as argued in his letter to Corning—would help the Union win the Civil War. As Lincoln recognized, without the power to punish those who deserted the army or those who encouraged others to desert, the Union would have been unable to maintain its force in numbers, certainly inhibiting its success. Indeed, the civil court system was wholly unable to prevent or punish desertion. Others similarly attribute the Union's success to Lincoln's suspension of the writ of habeas corpus and his willingness to try those detained before a military tribunal but for an altogether different reason. Historian Phillip Shaw Paludan surmises, "Lincoln kept the constitutional debate going throughout the war and thus propagandized to persuade the people that their constitutional system was adequate to survive and prosecute a war."[69] Lincoln, too, recognized the power of public sentiment as he had remarked during his famous debates with

Stephen A. Douglas that "public sentiment is everything."[70] In the end, Lincoln's army won, leaving a United States that "is" and not states that "are." Ultimately, Lincoln set a controversial precedent that would prove irresistible to his successors in later wars. The sixteenth president provided future wartime presidents with an invaluable tool: a brilliantly crafted, highly accessible, tightly reasoned legal argument justifying the military trial of insurrectionists or other enemy combatants. It was a masterpiece crafted by America's greatest lawyer-statesman when provoked by the City of Albany.

In 1866, the war having ended, the U.S. Supreme Court was called upon to consider the legality of Lincoln's suspension of habeas corpus and his use of military tribunals.[71] The Supreme Court, upon which Taney no longer sat, concluded, as Taney had in *Merryman*, that the president could not unilaterally suspend the writ of habeas corpus.

On October 5, 1864, the military commander for that military district arrested Lambdin P. Milligan, a lawyer and Indiana citizen, because the commander believed that Milligan was plotting to overthrow the government.[72] Although Milligan was not captured on the battlefield, a military commission tried him and sentenced him to death even though the civilian courts continued to function in Indiana.[73] Before his impending sentence was carried out, however, Milligan petitioned the Circuit Court of the United States for the District of Indiana for a writ of habeas corpus (107–9). The circuit court sent the question to the U.S. Supreme Court, which took over jurisdiction and issued the writ.

The Supreme Court reasoned that the suspension of habeas corpus was permissible but that such a suspension did not apply to Milligan's case because he had not joined the Confederate forces and was captured away from the battlefield in an area where civilian courts were still functioning. According to the court, Milligan was simply a person who was ideologically aligned with the Confederates and not an enemy combatant who should be tried by a military tribunal. Therefore, only the Indiana civilian courts could properly try Milligan. This postwar, post-Taney Court also impliedly validated Taney's opinion in *Merryman* as it agreed that only Congress may authorize the suspension of habeas corpus (127, 131).

Milligan made clear that the right of American citizens to seek a writ of habeas corpus may be suspended during wartime when those citizens join enemy forces or have been captured on the battlefield. Indeed, without such a ruling, "the Union could not have fought the Civil War, because the courts would have ordered President Lincoln to release thousands of Confederate POWs [prisoners of war] and spies."[74]

THE EMANCIPATION PROCLAMATION

E ven as a young lawyer in the nation's heartland, Abraham Lincoln understood that the promise of the Declaration of Independence rang hollow for the millions of black persons held in slavery. The single trait that Lincoln carried with him from the practice of law into the practice of politics was this underlying conviction. Perhaps his understanding of people, which deepened through the practice of law, solidified this belief in him. At first glance, his earliest statements and writings make him appear just another conservative Whig politician. Yet, his opposition to slavery was heroic and unusual. Unlike other politicians, such as Joshua Giddings, Lincoln did not make antislavery the centerpiece of his politics, and unlike others like William Henry Seward, he did not become publicly controversial for it. But he paid attention to the issue when others were trying to avoid it. For example, when in the Illinois legislature, he argued against slavery, and while in Congress, he supported the emancipation of slaves in Washington, D.C. As he later wrote to Albert G. Hodges in 1864, "I am naturally anti-slavery. If slavery is not wrong, nothing is wrong. I can not remember when I did not so think, and feel."[1]

In public, Lincoln opposed slavery even when taking that position was risky. After all, he lost the U.S. Senate seat he contested with Stephen A. Douglas in 1858. During their debates, Lincoln did not denounce Southerners for holding slaves, because his only solutions to the problem at that time—colonization, the idea that all or part of the African American population could be sent to settlements in either African or Central America, and freeing slaves and keeping them in a lower status—were unacceptable to them. But he did make clear his position against slavery with a forceful attack against the spread of slavery in America. He knew that he could not express a moral hatred of slavery so virulently that it would prevent him from ever taking additional steps against it.

When president-elect Lincoln boarded the inaugural train headed for Washington, the United States stood on the precipice of self-destruction—in the midst of a national crisis of unparalleled proportions. He set out to heal a country split by a deep racial chasm, so deep the founding fathers' dream of one new nation was unraveling thread by thread.

With eloquent confidence, Lincoln articulated his commitment to uniting a nation of people—black people and white people together. His ultimate message of equality still reverberates through the ages: "With malice toward none, with charity for all, with firmness in the right as God gives us to see the right, let us strive on to finish the work we are in, to bind up the nation's wounds, to care for him who shall have borne the battle and for his widow and his orphan, to do all which may achieve and cherish a just and lasting peace among ourselves and with all nations."[2] His message is one of genuine emancipation. The Emancipation Proclamation and the Thirteenth Amendment are the cornerstones of America's freedom foundation. With its ratification in December 1865, the Thirteenth Amendment gave final constitutional authority for the emancipation of approximately four million slaves. At the same time, the legal landscape of every slave state was irrevocably and instantly altered.

Almost from the beginning of his administration, abolitionists and Radical Republicans pressured Abraham Lincoln to issue an emancipation proclamation. In principle, Lincoln agreed with such a policy. His opposition to slavery came partly from a deep and personal repugnance. But always the consummate lawyer, Lincoln shaped his political policy with an eye toward his constitutional responsibility to preserve the Union. Early on in his administration, the political and philosophical line he drew in the vast American republic had allowed for the continuation of slavery in the South.

By allowing slave states to maintain the status quo until he secured their loyalty to the Union but by prohibiting the expansion of the institution into the territories, Lincoln believed that the ultimate result would be the extinction of slavery. He was shrewd in his strategic planning and postponed taking overt action against slavery until he believed he had wider support from the American public.

As a lawyer and politician, Lincoln had developed a fine judicious sense of timing. He had learned that some matters are best left alone. As a lawyer who fully understood the political context in which the law operates, Lincoln understood when to lead and when to let public opinion ripen. He was a master politician in the best sense of the term, understanding that leaders operate within a small window of opportunity. He knew when to seize the initiative and when to let matters develop. Inexperienced lawyers and those without political experience fail to appreciate this crucial dimension of successful democratic leadership.

Political timing was a factor in the date of Lincoln's issuance of the preliminary Emancipation Proclamation. "A blind man can see where the president's heart is," Frederick Douglass said.[3] But when Lincoln took office, he was no abolitionist; being an abolitionist was a position that was considered radical at the time and would only deny him political office. He had campaigned against the expansion of slavery into new states and territories, but he did not believe the Constitution allowed the federal government to eliminate it outright. He felt his oath of office would not permit it, either.

Lincoln had his reasons, of course, for avoiding the subject of slavery. The greatest good, he felt, was preserving the Union, and he knew the war would be lost before it began without the slaveholding Border States. "I hope to have God on my side," Lincoln said. "But I must have Kentucky."[4]

Lincoln also believed he was constitutionally bound as president to leave slavery alone. "If I could save the Union without freeing any slave I would do it, and if I could save it by freeing some and leaving others alone I would also do that," he wrote in a letter to Horace Greeley, *New York Tribune* editor. "I have here stated my purpose according to my view of official duty, and I intend no modification of my oft-expressed personal wish that all men everywhere could be free."[5]

Wishes are one thing, though, and actions another. More than anything what changed between the first year of the war, when Lincoln took no significant action against slavery, and the second, when he issued the Emancipation Proclamation on January 1, 1863, was the political climate. Lincoln himself would insist that he had not controlled events—that events controlled him.

From the beginning, Lincoln's paramount goal was to preserve the Union. Whether or not that mission included dismantling the institution of slavery depended upon what actions were necessary to save the Union. "I would save the Union. I would save it in the shortest way under the Constitution. . . . If there be those who would not save the Union, unless they could at the same time *save* slavery, I do not agree with them. If there be those who would not save the Union unless they could at the same time *destroy* slavery, I do not agree with them. My paramount object in this struggle *is* to save the Union, and is *not* either to save or to destroy slavery."[6] But because Lincoln as a lawyer was committed to the democratic process and the Constitution, he limited his early public criticisms to the expansion to slavery into the territories. Nevertheless, he increasingly articulated the dimensions of the nation's dilemma. In the last debate with Senator Douglas, Lincoln said, "[T]he debate about the extension of slavery represents the timeless struggle between right and wrong." As Lincoln came to confront the issue, he was able to articulate the issue for the public to understand it.

As the war unfolded, Lincoln came to recognize the importance of publicly denouncing the entire institution of slavery—not just its expansion. He understood that the struggle of black persons was very much the same struggle of every other human being—for selfhood and self-determination.

By mid-summer 1862, he was openly discussing the issue with several of his cabinet members. He came to believe that military law and political necessity now required the emancipation of slaves by an executive order. On July 22, Lincoln read a rough draft of an Emancipation Proclamation to his cabinet. Francis B. Carpenter, the artist who painted the famous portrait of Lincoln and his cabinet discussing the proclamation, called the meeting "a scene second only in historical importance and interest to that of the Declaration of Independence."[7] Taking the advice of Secretary of State Seward, Lincoln waited for a military victory before making his proclamation public: "I do not want to issue a document that the whole world . . . must necessarily see as inoperative, like the Pope's bull against the comet."[8]

In 1862, however, the timing was right for one of Lincoln's greatest acts of political courage. After the Battle of Antietam, a Union victory—albeit a costly one with total casualties exceeding twenty-six thousand in one horrifying day—he understood it was time to act. Already expecting heavy criticism for leaning toward emancipation, Lincoln knew that if the Union army's fortunes took another turn for the worse, he could easily miss the opportunity to act. With something resembling a victory, he could push ahead. The cries of Radical Republicans and governors who wanted an end to slavery had risen to fever pitch, and, seemingly, sentiment was turning their way. Even facing congressional midterm elections, he felt the time was ripe to act.

On September 22, 1862, five days after the Union victory at Antietam, Lincoln issued the preliminary Emancipation Proclamation: "And by virtue of the power, and for the purpose aforesaid, I do order and declare that all persons held as slaves within said designated States and, parts of States, are, and henceforward shall be free; and that the Executive Government of the United States, including the military and naval authorities thereof, will recognize and maintain the freedom of said persons."[9] Until this point in his presidency, Lincoln had viewed the Civil War as a rebellion, a fight to preserve the Union without addressing the institution of slavery. But by issuing the preliminary Emancipation Proclamation, Lincoln threatened to crush the Confederacy by destroying slavery, the basis of its economy and society. Some in the North, on the other hand, were waging a moral crusade to free the slaves. It was the first time in American history when war aims were changed in the middle of war.

But the Emancipation Proclamation also illustrates Lincoln's concentric legal and political grasp of issues. The problem was prodigious. Nothing in the Constitution authorized the Congress or the president to confiscate property without compensation. When the time came for the final Emancipation Proclamation on New Year's Day 1863, Lincoln had determined that his act was a war measure taken as commander in chief to weaken the enemy.

The public could understand the basic legal arguments that under the law, slaves were property—the valuation of each slave written next to his or her name in the tax assessors' books—and as commander in chief, Lincoln had the authority to seize the property of insurgents to quell rebellion. His action exemplifies a lawyer-statesman who consistently took the shortest distance between two legal points. He saw the problem with the same logical directness with which he saw most problems: A commander in chief may under military necessity take property. Slaves are property. Because there was military necessity, he argued, the commander in chief could take the property.

"Reading the Emancipation Proclamation," engraved by J. W. Watts, after work by H. W. Herrick, copyright 1864, Lucius Stebbins, published by S. A. Peters, Hartford, Connecticut. The proclamation, a war measure, invited former slaves to serve in the Union army and navy. There could be no return to bondage. By drawing them to the Union's cause, the proclamation would simultaneously strengthen the North's war effort and weaken that of its Confederate opponent. Courtesy of the Frank and Virginia Williams Collection of Lincolniana.

Those slaves freed by the proclamation would "be received into the armed service of the United States to garrison forts, positions, stations, and other places."[10] In this way, Lincoln addressed manpower shortages with a new source of soldiers, "the great available and as yet unavailed of, force for the restoration of the Union." Nearly two hundred thousand African Americans would serve under arms to help end the rebellion.

While the document was crafted as a military order, it had all of the attributes of a legal and political statement, too. Lincoln's keen understanding of law and politics allowed him to reason to broader principles rather than limit himself to precedent. His democratic values always allowed him to consider alternate interpretations. When Lincoln spoke on the issue of equality, he did so with passion and conviction: "Let us discard all this quibbling about this man and the other man, this race and that race and the other race being inferior, and therefore they must be placed in an inferior position. Let us discard all these things and unite as one people throughout this land, until we shall once more stand up declaring that all men are created equal."[11]

Consider his logic regarding the question of slavery. In a piece of Lincoln's writing from 1854 is an example of his legal reasoning, written at a time when slavery was still solidly legal in many areas of the country and the infamous *Dred Scott v. Sandford* decision was working its way through the courts.[12] Like any good lawyer, Lincoln grounded his action on two legally tenable premises of the time. The first, which was morally reprehensible to him but which the Supreme Court in 1857 had affirmed the *Dred Scott v. Sandford* decision, was that slaves were property. The second was that the president constitutionally may take property under military necessity without providing compensation. Again, Lincoln's justification reveals nothing about his own thoughts on slavery; rather, it demonstrates his appreciation that the circumstances of the war demanded a simpler rationalization.

Not everyone supported the proclamation, and Lincoln was quick to rebut their arguments. To one critic, James C. Conkling, the president made clear the resolve behind his order, as he wrote on August 26, 1863: "You dislike the emancipation proclamation; and, perhaps, would have it retracted. You say it is unconstitutional—

I think differently. I think the constitution invests its commander-in-chief, with the law of war, in time of war. The most that can be said, if so much, is, that slaves are property. Is there—has there ever been—any question that by the law of war, property, both of enemies and friends, may be taken when needed? And is it not needed whenever taking it, helps us, or hurts the enemy?" Lincoln saw the slavery problems with the same logical directness with which he saw most problems. A commander-in-chief may, under military necessity, take property. Slaves are property. There is a military necessity, so the commander-in-chief proclaims that the property is taken. Lincoln's legal logic is also evident in his letter to Conkling: "You say you will not fight to free negroes. Some of them seem willing to fight for you; but, no matter. Fight you, then, exclusively to save the Union. . . . Whenever you shall have conquered all resistance to the Union, if I shall urge you to continue fighting, it will be an apt time, then, for you to declare you will not fight to free negroes."[13]

Black Americans hailed Lincoln as a hero for they knew that freedom was on the horizon. Word quickly spread that there was an administration in Washington that finally supported and welcomed emancipation. Something as hopeful and dramatic as freedom cannot be contained. Thousands of slaves, even in territory still controlled by the Confederacy, fled to the protection of the Union lines. A former Alabama slave, Wallace Turnage, who in the nineteenth century wrote an account of his years in slavery, recalled his escape in 1864 in a rowboat on Mobile Bay in Virginia. When rescued in rough weather by a Union gunboat, he stated, "I now dread the gun and handcuffs and pistols no more. Nor the blewing [sic] of horns and running of hounds; nor the threats of death from the rebel's authority. I can now speak my opinion to men of all grades and colors, and no one to question my right to speak."[14]

With support of the administration, thousands of slaves had walked, run, or rowed to freedom by February 1865. This perceived "mass exodus" caused some people great trepidation as evidenced by Attorney General Edward Bates's reply to a letter from A. W. Bradford, Maryland governor: "I am honored with your letter of yesterday informing me that large numbers of slaves owned in Maryland, are

daily making their way into the District of Columbia from the neigh-
boring counties of your State, which you assure me is producing great
anxiety and complaint in your community. . . . In these distempered
times, I am not at all surprised to hear that Slaves in the border States
are using all available means to escape into free territory."[15]

No matter how many slaves were actually freed under the auspices
of the Emancipation Proclamation, what proved essential to the war
was that Lincoln, by issuing it, made slave liberation a goal of the
Union government. Not only did emancipation begin removing the
useful labor of black workers from the home front Confederacy but it
also added more labor power to the Union cause. Even though Lincoln
described emancipation as a necessary war measure, he also showed
political shrewdness by making it a policy of his administration.

Official liberty for the slaves came in December 1865 with the
ratification of the Thirteenth Amendment to the Constitution forever
abolishing slavery. Lincoln had vigorously supported the Thirteenth
Amendment, insisting that it be a part of the National Union Party
platform for the 1864 election. The effect of the Thirteenth Amendment validated his dedication to freedom and the belief that American democracy is the last best hope of earth.

In his annual message to Congress in December 1862, Lincoln had
recommended the adoption of three constitutional amendments directed at the abolition of slavery. The first proposed amendment offered
federal funds to any state "wherein slavery now exists, which shall abolish
the same therein, at any time, or times, before the first day of January,
in the year of our Lord one thousand and nine hundred."[16] The second
proposed amendment guaranteed "all slaves who shall have enjoyed
actual freedom by the chances of the war, at any time before the end of
the rebellion, shall be forever free; but all owners of such, who shall not
have been disloyal, shall be compensated for them."[17] The third proposed
amendment authorized federal funds for voluntary colonization.

Voluntary colonization would mean that African Americans would
of their own choice move to settlements in Africa or Central America.
Colonization was, in many ways, an out-of-sight, out-of-mind so-
lution. This was an idea Lincoln had earlier articulated. Even while
eulogizing his political hero Henry Clay in 1852, Lincoln referenced

colonization: "There is a moral fitness in the idea of returning to Africa her children whose ancestors have been torn away from her by the ruthless hand of fraud and violence."[18] In his address to a committee of black leaders on August 14, 1862, Lincoln urged African American leaders to take advantage of $600,000 in congressional appropriations to fund colonization in Africa and the Caribbean.[19] The president had invited five African Americans to the White House to hear their views on colonization. On that August afternoon, Lincoln told the men seated before him that Congress had recently appropriated a sum of money to colonize freed slaves. "Why should they leave this country?" the president asked rhetorically. He continued to provide them with an answer: "You and we are different races. We have between us a broader difference than exists between almost any other two races. Whether it is right or wrong I need not discuss, but this physical difference is a great disadvantage to us both, as I think your race suffer very greatly, many of them by living among us, while ours suffer from your presence. In a word we suffer on each side. If this is admitted, it affords a reason at least why we should be separated. You here are free men I suppose."[20]

A voice among them replied "Yes, sir" to the president's rhetorical question. Lincoln told them, "Your race are suffering, in my judgment, the greatest wrong inflicted on any people" (5:372). Nevertheless, he asked them to consider whether removing their classification as slaves would really place them on equal grounds with the white race. In Lincoln's estimation, it would not.

Lincoln urged the men to consider supporting colonization.

I need not recount to you the effects upon white men, growing out of the institution of Slavery. . . . See our present condition—the country engaged in war!—our white men cutting one another's throats, none knowing how far it will extend. . . . But for your race among us there could not be war, although many men engaged on either side do not care for you one way or the other. Nevertheless, I repeat, without the institution of Slavery and the colored race as a basis, the war could not have an existence. It is better for us both, therefore, to be separated. (5:372)

Lincoln pointed, for an example, to the successes in the colony of Liberia, with a population of three hundred thousand to four hundred thousand, including twelve thousand American slaves who had settled there upon being freed. Recognizing that African Americans might not want to settle as far away as Africa, Lincoln offered an alternative: "The place I am thinking about having for a colony is in Central America. . . . The country is a very excellent one for any people, and with great natural resources and advantages, and especially because of the similarity of climate with your native land—thus being suited to your physical condition." He described for them all that such a colony would have to offer them:

> The particular place I have in view is to be a great highway from the Atlantic or Caribbean Sea to the Pacific Ocean, and this particular place has all the advantages for a colony. On both sides there are harbors among the finest in the world. Again, there is evidence of very rich coal mines. A certain amount of coal is valuable in any country, and there may be more than enough for the wants of the country. Why I attach so much importance to coal is, it will afford an opportunity to the inhabitants for immediate employment till they get ready to settle permanently in their homes. (5:373–74)

Lincoln asked the men to consider the idea and to help him get "a number of able-bodied men, with their wives and children, who are willing to go" and join the government's colonization efforts. Lincoln thought that his plan would work so long as he could find "twenty-five able-bodied men, with a mixture of women and children" who were willing to go (5:375). The president's remarks, which a reporter present recorded, were printed in the *New York Tribune* the next day, and, not surprising, the newspaper heavily criticized them, as it was widely believed that colonization was cost prohibitive.

Lincoln took a long time before he lost interest in this scheme. His 1862 address that included his proposed colonization amendment was given only one month before he issued the final Emancipation Proclamation.

In closing his address to Congress that December, Lincoln made these prophetic remarks: "Fellow-citizens, *we* cannot escape history. We of this Congress and this administration, will be remembered in spite of ourselves. No personal significance, or insignificance, can spare one or another of us. The fiery trial through which we pass, will light us down, in honor or dishonor, to the latest generation. We *say* we are for the Union. The world will not forget that we say this. We know how to save the Union. The world knows we do know how to save it. We—even *we here*—hold the power, and bear the responsibility. In *giving* freedom to the *slave*, we *assure* freedom to the *free*—honorable alike in what we give and what we preserve. We shall nobly save, or meanly lose, the last best, hope of earth."[21]

The ultimate failure of colonization in America may have been due to Lincoln's own maneuvering. It is possible that his public actions were a way to prepare the white population for his emancipation policy, which would abolish slavery altogether. That is, by advocating colonization in his annual messages and publicly, it might make the Emancipation Proclamation more acceptable to those who resisted it in the North. Historian Don E. Fehrenbacher suggests "that Lincoln's support of colonization . . . became during his presidential years a calculated, dissimulative strategy aimed primarily at the white mind rather than the black population—in other words, that he hoped for nothing more than a token emigration of blacks to relieve some of the racial fears engendered by the thought of emancipation."[22]

By the time the Emancipation Proclamation was issued, colonization was no longer supported, although Lincoln continued to speak of it as one option to the problem that had for some time plagued the nation. An editorial in the *New York Tribune* read:

> No one who has not thoughtfully and carefully and earnestly considered President Lincoln's proclamation will be likely to realize how admirable and comprehensive are its suggestions, and how surely their adoption will conduce to national integrity and internal peace. Look for a moment at the question of negro expatriation, which is one of the chief difficulties of our position. There are many worthy and good men, and ten

times more of the other sort, who hold, that whenever slavery is abolished the negro should be sent out of the country. We have much charity for this opinion, for we once held it, but we are now convinced that it is an error. That the negro race, wherever free, will gradually migrate southward, colonizing the less populous West Indies, Central America, and the adjacent portions of South America, we believe. Climate, soil, natural products, ease of obtaining a rude yet ample subsistence, and the ready fraternisation of blacks with the Indian and mongrel races who now exist in those regions, and who are nowise above our Southern negroes in the social scale, not even in their own opinion, will all attract them that way. But if slavery were ended tomorrow, we are confident that even South Carolina would be in no hurry to expel from her soil the most industrious and productive half of her people; that portion amongst whom drunkards and profligates are scarce, while its office-seekers, bar-room loungers, and pot-house brawlers have yet to be developed. A State can spare its idlers far better than its workers, and it is only from dread of their influence on the slaves that a slave-holding people ever desire the expulsion of their free blacks. Were slavery dead this day, even the Carolina aristocracy would prefer, as labourers on the plantations, the negroes to whom they are accustomed, and whose manners are respectful and submissive, to any immigrants by whom they could be promptly replaced. It is quite likely that in time white labour would demonstrate its superior energy and intelligence by driving out the black. But for the present the Carolina planters would generally hire their ex-slaves more satisfactorily to themselves than they could replace them from any quarter.[23]

Despite one's position in a debate on Lincoln's methods, there can be no dispute that he accomplished what he set out to do. He saved the Union. By issuing the Emancipation Proclamation, Lincoln ran the first leg in a long relay toward full equality. And his early run on racial segregation set the stage for later emendations to the Constitution, namely the Thirteenth, Fourteenth, and Fifteenth Amendments.

THE ASSASSINATION AND
APOTHEOSIS OF A HERO

England's Prime Minister Stanley Baldwin once observed: "Contemporary judgments were illusory; look at Lincoln's case, how in his lifetime he was thought to be a clumsy lumbering countryman, blundering along without knowing where he was going. Since his death his significance has grown steadily."[1] Many great heroes, including the likes of Socrates, Galileo Galilei, and Vincent van Gogh, were shunned and criticized during their lifetimes, and Lincoln is no exception. Tragically, in many cases, it is not until death has robbed the world of its heroes that the world celebrates their greatness.

Regicide, the death of any sitting chief executive, invariably generates a deep and enduring impact on the citizenry. Personal shock quickly gives way to public anxiety, fueled by a bombardment of news and pictures of the tragedy that keep nightmarish memories vividly and profoundly alive. Americans who live through such traumas are virtually lurched from the abyss of political apathy. By contrast, deaths of other leaders, political and national alike, seem to inspire only momentary ripples in the public consciousness. The pervasive mourning triggered by the violent death of incumbent presidents—from Lincoln to James Garfield to William McKinley to John F. Kennedy—proves that the resident of the White House occupies a unique place in the collective American psyche. Presidents are more than authority figures; they are the living "fathers" of their country.

The first—and still the most wrenching—of these national calamities was the murder of Abraham Lincoln only days after the Union had achieved victory in the long and bloody Civil War. The murder of Abraham Lincoln on Good Friday, April 14, 1865, struck the American psyche like a hammer blow. No previous president had been assassinated (though three have been killed since). Lincoln died at the successful conclusion of an Armageddon that finally reconciled the living nation's values with those enshrined in the Declaration of Independence, so mass shock and mourning were surely not surprising. To America, Lincoln's murder seemed so gratuitous, so irrational, and so utterly un-American that it defied logic. The nation had just endured a brutal, punishing four-year war, and just as the tide had begun to turn, in the midst of widespread national rejoicing at the restoration of peace, Lincoln's assassination was a sharp reminder of the harrowing days of war. As historian Allan Nevins comments, Lincoln's slaying "was clearly a sequel of the war, a product of its senseless hatreds, fears and cruelties."[2]

Abraham Lincoln was acutely aware that he was an assassination target. Like Kennedy one hundred years later, he sometimes mused over the possibility of his death. On the day he was shot, Lincoln remarked to William Crook, his bodyguard, "I believe there are men who want to take my life. And I have no doubt they will do it."[3] Despite these mounting beliefs, it was Lincoln's belief that human beings all have a "right to rise," and that principle forbade an imperial presidency. Lincoln, who disliked guards and panoply, once said he could not be the people's president if he shut himself up for safety in an iron box and that an assassin had better be careful because he might get somebody worse for the next president.

Lincoln had been aware of the mobbing and killing of Elijah P. Lovejoy in 1837, when Lovejoy defended his abolitionist newspaper in Alton, Illinois, and, by dying at the hands of angry proslavery men, gave the cause its first martyr. Lovejoy's death was the issue stressed by Abraham Lincoln in his Springfield, Illinois, Lyceum speech.

> At what point shall we expect the approach of danger? By what means shall we fortify against it? Shall we expect some

transatlantic military giant, to step the Ocean, and crush us at a blow? Never! . . .

At what point then is the approach of danger to be expected? I answer, if it ever reach us, it must spring up amongst us. It cannot come from abroad. If destruction be our lot, we must ourselves be its author and finisher. As a nation of freemen, we must live through all time, or die by suicide.

I hope I am over wary; but if I am not, there is, even now, something of ill-omen, amongst us. I mean the increasing disregard for law which pervades the country; the growing disposition to substitute the wild and furious passions, in lieu of the sober judgment of Courts; and the worse than savage mobs, for the executive ministers of justice.[4]

It is perhaps these fearless beliefs that led to Lincoln's ultimate demise, but it is his strength in conviction that makes him a hero today. Scholar Harold Holzer observes, Lincoln "had died for the American sin of slavery, a sacrifice for national resurrection; as in Leviticus, he had proclaimed liberty throughout the land, leading 'all the inhabitants thereof' from bondage in the promised land of freedom."[5]

From 1861 to 1865, America had come to know killing too well. The nation—North and South—was calloused to war's brutalities, to civil disorders (the Draft Riots in New York in 1863 killed or wounded almost a thousand), to brutalities in prison camps, to the savagery of guerilla raids, to the terrible slaughter on the battlefield. Callous, also, to military rule.

After the first years of defeats, the North's material and manpower—along with the maturing federal generals and admirals—prevailed. On April 11, Lincoln addressed a crowd on the White House lawn. He carefully laid out a plan for the reunion of the states. His tone was conciliatory. John Wilkes Booth, listening, was outraged. He muttered to an accomplice that that was the last speech Lincoln would make. He hated this "Abe," this "Emperor" who wanted to install democracy. Lincoln actually had been to Booth's precious Richmond, Virginia, had entered the conquered capital on April 4. Before that, he had been elected again, and Booth had been there on

March 4 to watch him make that sickening inaugural speech about "malice toward none and charity for all."[6] It was clear to Booth that Lincoln would not really "bind up the nation's wounds."[7] With Lee defeated, Booth believed that Lincoln must be killed. As Booth put it in his April 13 diary entry, "Until today, nothing was ever thought of sacrificing to our country's wrongs. For six months we had worked to capture, but our cause being almost lost, something decisive and great must be done."[8]

This decision to kill Lincoln was not Booth's first plot against the president. Before, he had wanted to kidnap Lincoln and exchange him for the thousands of Confederate prisoners General Robert E. Lee

"President Lincoln Riding through Richmond, Va., April 4th, 1865."
After the Confederate evacuation of Richmond and unlike this engraving appearing in *Frank Leslie's Illustrated History of the Civil War*, President Lincoln walked the streets of the former Confederate capital accompanied by only a small detachment of sailors. Everywhere the president was besieged by emancipated slaves who, to his discomfort, fell on their knees. Courtesy of the Frank and Virginia Williams Collection of Lincolniana.

so desperately needed back in his armies. For that, Booth had assembled and subsidized a vaudeville troop of conspirators. He had some money, charm, and contacts. Booth first planned to seize the president at Ford's Theatre during the performance of *Jack Cade* on January 18, 1865. He knew Lincoln went often to the theater. Indeed, in 1863, the president had seen Booth at Ford's in *The Marble Heart* and had admired his acting. That was the year Booth took to denouncing Lincoln's administration from the stage—an act that got him arrested in Saint Louis, Missouri, and released only when he signed an oath of allegiance to the Union.[9]

While no evidence exists that Lincoln was aware of this plot, he certainly knew someone was after him. On March 19, 1864, the *New York Times* reported rumors of a plan, vetoed by Confederate President Jefferson Davis, to send 150 Confederate raiders to kidnap Lincoln. In August of that year, a sniper plugged the president's top hat as he rode the three miles from the White House to his summer retreat at the Soldiers' Home. Unabashed, Lincoln rode in and told the retreat's sentry, "Someone seems to have tried killing me."[10]

Next came a report in November from Union spies that Confederates in Montreal were plotting Lincoln's death (Booth was then in New York, fresh from a Canadian visit, playing Marc Antony in *Julius Caesar* with his brothers Edwin and Junius Brutus Jr.). On December 1, 1864, an unsigned ad appeared in the Selma, Alabama, *Dispatch* soliciting funds to arrange the murders of Lincoln, Vice President Andrew Johnson, and Secretary of State William Henry Seward. By April 1865, Lincoln had numerous serious death threats filed in his desk.

Luke P. Blackburn, Kentucky physician and member of the Confederates' Canadian operation, proposed to kill Lincoln by infecting him with yellow fever. Blackburn purchased several expensive shirts, which had been exposed to clothing taken from several victims who died of yellow fever. Blackburn intended to deliver the shirts as a gift, thereby exposing Lincoln to the dreaded disease. The plot failed when Blackburn's agent declined to deliver the shirts. Unknown to medicine at the time, yellow fever was not an infectious disease.[11]

Naturally, these reports brought efforts to protect the president, despite his dislike for bodyguards. Soon after taking office in 1862,

Edwin M. Stanton had had his national executive police take over patrolling Washington from the small, badly manned metropolitan police. But this national executive police did not guard the president. That was left to special detachments of cavalry. Lincoln complained that their jangling prevented conversation in his carriage. Also, bodyguards were either detailed by the metropolitan police or chosen by Lincoln's old friend Ward Hill Lamon, U.S. Marshall of the District of Columbia. Altogether, it was catch-as-catch-can.

Next, Booth planned to kidnap the president on March 20, 1865. Booth and his group abandoned its plans. Booth and Lewis Paine supposedly lay in wait for Lincoln near the White House. They were frightened away when Lincoln strolled into view surrounded by a crowd of men.[12]

On March 13, Booth reassembled his band at Mrs. Mary Surratt's Washington boardinghouse. On March 18, Booth learned that Lincoln would be going to the Soldiers' Home. Again the conspirators gathered. By the lonely road they waited. The carriage clattered into view, alone. The conspirators saw that it was not Lincoln in the carriage, rather the Chief Justice of the United States, Salmon P. Chase. The conspirators scattered. On Saturday, April 8, Booth checked into the National Hotel, Washington. On the tenth, he heard shouts in the street that told him that Lee had surrendered at Appomattox. Drinking heavily, he called at Mrs. Surratt's searching for remnants of his gang. After listening to Lincoln's gentle speech on the eleventh of April, Booth railed about votes for black persons and drank on. Like assassins of a later era—Oswald, Ray, Sirhan—he now seemed bent on mad public displays of his opinions (42–49).

Lincoln not only spoke of his premonitions of death—he saw himself dead. Within a month before April 14, he remarked on a dream in which he saw a corpse lying in state in the East Room. The dreaming president asked a guard who it was that lay dead in the White House. He answered, "The President; he was killed by an assassin." Surely, this was in the president's mind on the fourteenth when he conducted his 11:00 A.M. cabinet meeting. He listened once more to Stanton's urgings that parts of the defeated South be put under military rule and denied statehood. In the afternoon, Lincoln went to the War Department and requested that Major Thomas Eckert accompany him as bodyguard to the theater that night (42–49).

Stanton denied the request.

After the fatal shot was fired in Ford's Theatre, on Good Friday, April 14, 1865, confusion set in. Dr. Charles Leale, a twenty-three-year-old assistant army surgeon, ordered the president placed on the floor and examined the wounded chief executive. Finding blood on the back of Lincoln's head, Leale searched and found the hole made by Booth's attack. Concluding that the bullet was in the president's brain, Leale realized the president had been mortally wounded (42–49).

Some on the scene urged that the president be taken back to the White House, but Leale insisted that he could not survive the trip. It was then decided to move Lincoln to a dwelling nearby. At virtually the same moment, young Henry Safford, a tenant in William Petersen's house across from Ford's Theatre on Tenth Street, heard noises from the street, opened his window, and shouted, "What's the matter?" (42–49).

"The President has been shot" came the answer. Safford cried, "Bring him in here." Commanded to "take me to your best room," Safford led the way to a small sleeping compartment, 9½ feet by 17 feet, at the back of the first floor hall, occupied at the time by one William T. Clark, a soldier on leave who was not in his room at the time the president arrived (42–49).

The president's 6'4" frame required that he be laid diagonally on the bed. Lincoln's head was propped up so he could breathe more easily. Officials began gathering around the bedside, beginning a vigil later described to artist Hermann Faber, who sketched the scene only a few hours after Lincoln's death. In all, fifty-five individuals visited the dying president's bedside (42–49).

By this time, Dr. Joseph K. Barnes, the Surgeon General of the Army, had joined several other doctors at the scene. All they could do, however, was try to keep Lincoln warm, administer occasional stimulants, put the then-popular mustard plaster on his chest, and keep the wound open and free of blood clots to prevent pressure from building up inside his brain. In this condition, Lincoln lingered for almost nine excruciating hours before he drew his last breath (42–49).

Lincoln died at 7:22 A.M. on Saturday, April 15. Throughout America, weeping women, angry men, and rabid mobs poured out to lament and protest the act. This is not what Booth expected or hoped. Even the Richmond *Whig* wrote, "The heaviest blow which has ever fallen upon the people of the South has descended."[13]

On that day, America changed forever. A citizen of this great nation had murdered his president. As Springfield's *Illinois State Register* said on April 15, "The effect of this terrible blow cannot now be estimated."[14] While it was easy enough to yoke the South in recompense for Booth's mad act, it was less easy to regain innocence. In the years that followed, Americans found it was lost forever in the mystery of themselves. The first assassination was the hardest. After Lincoln, Americans knew how. As Benjamin Disraeli said of Lincoln's death on May 10, 1865, "Assassination has never changed the history of the world."[15]

Gone suddenly was the leader who had patiently guided the Union to victory, deftly steered a government roiled by unprecedented challenge, inspired a people through the most perilous crisis in the nation's history, and established black freedom. Those who continued to hate Lincoln remained silent, creating the appearance that mourning for him was universal.[16]

Stanton delivered the final benediction in the room of the president's death.

"Now," Stanton said, "he belongs to the ages."

Stanton's eloquent summation suggests that fate, in the end, allowed Lincoln to define both his life and his death. Stanton's echo from that day has helped inspire subsequent generations to come to terms with Lincoln's leadership and character.

Lincoln's path to sainthood was further assured because he was assassinated on Good Friday, dying suddenly and violently and not at home in bed as George Washington had in 1799. Printmakers seemed to believe that the public preferred its fallen leaders to die in places worthy of their exalted positions, and this perception encouraged them to enhance and embellish the place where Lincoln expired. They ignored, in large part, that the people recognized—and appreciated—the symmetry and humility consistent with greatness in a president who was born in a log cabin and who died in a simple boardinghouse.

Within eight hours after the president's death, "Republican congressmen in secret caucus agreed that his death was a Godsend to their cause," because successor Andrew Johnson of Tennessee was expected to punish Southerners in ways that Lincoln was resisting.[17] Johnson was a pro-war Democrat with limited political skills, undisguised racial prejudices, and implacable loyalty to state sovereignty

Public sentiment, however, quickly stymied this perception. Instead, "[p]oliticians of all parties were apparently startled by the extent of the national grief over Lincoln, and, politician-like, they decided to capitalize on it." The following February saw a joint session of Congress commemorating the Emancipator's birth. Historian George Bancroft offered praise, extolling Lincoln as a leader who was molded by events rather than one who shapes the times in accordance with his own will.[18]

Even Lincoln could never have solved all the problems of the postwar years. His untimely death, however, robbed the nation of this prospect. The president's death in office assured the unchecked ascendancy of racism while also posthumously guaranteeing the near-beatification of Lincoln as the secular saint who had saved democracy.

A GREAT AMERICAN HERO

When America became an independent nation in 1776, the founding fathers provided the country with a unique sense of identity. It would be established not on a common faith, language, or ethnicity but on a set of beliefs and democratic values. They believed in opportunity, liberty, and the right to rise on the basis of hard work. Through their own perseverance, courage, brilliance, and ingenuity, they became the first American heroes. Although the founding fathers had crafted the Constitution and laid down the foundation for the American experiment, it was up to successors to give meaning to these principles.

Twenty-five years after the signing of the Declaration of Independence, John Marshall took the bench as the fourth Chief Justice of the United States. He shared many of the same characteristics as the founders, and his strength and political courage have led many to regard him as a founding father, too. In his broad national perspective, he bestowed the judicial branch with power and authority and ensured the realization of the founders' vision—the coexistence of three separate but coequal branches of government. He also recognized the insight of the founders and gave meaning to some of the most important constitutional provisions: the necessary-and-proper clause and the supremacy clause. The first clause, Article I, Section 8, gave Congress great authority to legislate broadly. In 1819, in *McCulloch v. Maryland*, Chief Justice John Marshall upheld the constitutionality of the legislation creating Second Bank of the United States as permitted under this clause. In the supremacy clause, Article VI, permitted and required judicial review by state judges for constitutional questions.

Twenty-six years after Marshall's death, a new hero, Abraham Lincoln, took the oath of office as America's sixteenth president to "preserve, protect and defend the Constitution of the United States." Throughout his presidency, Lincoln recognized the importance of the Constitution's democratic principles. Not only did Lincoln uphold the meaning of the Constitution but he also fought to honor the founders' ideas that formed the impetus behind the Constitution. As commander in chief during the Civil War, he led the country in a civil war not only to preserve the Union that the founders fought to create but also to end slavery and ensure equality for all, as some envisioned it. As Paul Johnson observes, "Lincoln was able to inaugurate [a] new kind of heroic leadership in American history because he was a new kind of American—someone for whom citizenship of the union was far more important than his provenance from a particular state."[1]

"Union," colored engraving, by H. S. Sadd from a painting by T. H. Matteson, published by William Pate, 1862. Lincoln's qualities placed him in America's pantheon of heroes, even eclipsing Henry Clay (seated center), "his beau ideal of a statesman." The president's words and actions led America through the Civil War and galvanized the nation's courage. Courtesy of the Frank and Virginia Williams Collection of Lincolniana.

Like Marshall, Lincoln was not always popular and was in many ways controversial, but this is commonly the experience of heroes. Heroes become great by thinking outside the box, testing the limits and, often, evoking change. In a society that resists change, it is difficult for heroes to achieve greatness and popularity for having evoked change, but, posthumously, Lincoln, like Marshall, was able to do just that.

Lincoln furthered the country in its quest for independence and democratic value. Lincoln is a hero not only by the standards of his day but by today's standards as well. He embodies political courage when he stood up to secession and fought to preserve America's great democratic experiment. With resolve, Lincoln led the country through the Civil War, not only to preserve the nation but also in the process to abolish slavery. During the nation's darkest hour, he issued the Emancipation Proclamation, the first and most important measure toward universal freedom. Lincoln scholar Allen C. Guelzo observes, "The Emancipation Proclamation was the most revolutionary pronouncement ever signed by an American president, striking the legal shackles from four million black slaves and setting the nation's face toward the total abolition of slavery within three more years."[2]

Although more than two hundred years have passed since Abraham Lincoln's birth, he still remains the leader who defined democratic government at Gettysburg, the commander in chief who preserved America's greatest experiment by winning the Civil War, and the chief executive who is continually ranked highest among all American presidents. He has become a mythic figure in the deepest sense of the word and is best remembered for two great acts—his preservation of the Union and his abolishment of slavery through the Emancipation Proclamation, which supported what became the Thirteenth Amendment. It was a war that eradicated the institution of slavery and created the idea of nationhood. In his 1863 Gettysburg Address, Lincoln captured the spirit of the war and the cause for which he and the Union soldiers were fighting so relentlessly. He proclaimed that "this nation, under God, shall have a new birth of freedom—and that government of the people, by the people, for the

"Lincoln at Gettysburg," 1863, print after a painting by Fletcher Ransom.
This image idealizes Abraham Lincoln redefining the country from
"the United States are" to "the United States is," thus making a nation.
Courtesy of the Frank and Virginia Williams Collection of Lincolniana.

people, shall not perish from the earth." The timeless phrase "government of the people, by the people, for the people" has resonated far
beyond Gettysburg, Pennsylvania. Lincoln was mistaken when he
predicted "the world will little note, nor long remember what we say
here."[3] Instead, these words captured the definition of democracy in
the United States.[4]

The circumstances of his life and his legacy, time and again, transcend his era. And it is because of this legacy that the world still
talks about Lincoln and his greatness. To paraphrase biographer Carl
Sandburg, millions of people outside the United States also take him
for their own. Lincoln belongs to them, too. He was a personal treasure who had something they "would like to see spread everywhere
over the world." Sandburg told Congress on the 150th anniversary of
Lincoln's birth: "Democracy? We cannot find the words to say exactly
what it is, but Lincoln had it. In his blood and bones he carried it. In
the breath of his speeches and writings it is there. . . . Government

where the people have the say-so, one way or another telling their elected leaders what they want. He had the idea. He embodied it. It is there in the lights and shadows of his personality."[5]

The name Abraham Lincoln will live always wherever liberty and freedom are revered. He had a focused sense of justice and a great respect for the mandates of both the Declaration of Independence and the Constitution, and he also knew that without a true dedication to preserving these United States as *united* states, the founders' democratic experiment would fail. Lincoln guided the country through hard-fought struggles that ensured the sanctity of the Constitution and its principles. It is his strength, his political courage, and his ability to do what is right in the face of adversity that make him revered today. Whether it was as president, lawyer, or schoolboy, Lincoln always exemplified the foundational virtues of American society: character, leadership, justice, and a commitment to excellence in whatever one endeavors. It is those qualities that make him a hero today.

ACKNOWLEDGMENTS

This book could not have been written without the invaluable assistance of my former law clerk and research assistant Nicole Benjamin. To her I owe much as I do William D. Pederson, who gave the manuscript a good read, offering many valuable suggestions. Harold Holzer's friendship and support were invaluable. Series editors Sylvia Frank Rodrigue, Sara Vaughn Gabbard, and Richard W. Etulain have been extremely supportive. I am also appreciative of the late David M. Rich, who, until his death, catalogued the books and pamphlets of the Frank and Virginia Williams Collection of Lincolniana, and of Alfred Calebetta, who has catalogued everything else, including photographs and prints. He assisted with the illustrations herein, which are all from the Frank and Virginia Williams Collection of Lincolniana.

Of course, my wife of forty-six years, Virginia Williams, has used her indomitable spirit and positive reinforcement to keep me going.

Any mistakes here are my own.

RECENT BOOKS ON ABRAHAM LINCOLN

In 1893, Frederick Douglass declared, "It is impossible for . . . anybody . . . to say anything new about Abraham Lincoln," yet historians and authors continue to achieve the impossible.[1] February 12, 2009, marked the bicentennial of Abraham Lincoln's birth, and the grand celebrations provided a chance to contemplate the ongoing study of his life and legacy. The books listed here address, impliedly or overtly, Abraham Lincoln's heroic qualities. Although none of them use "hero" as a theme, their rich contents help describe why so many believe Abraham Lincoln is the quintessential American hero.

In the 1960s, the *Guinness Book of Records* reported that more books had been written about Abraham Lincoln than any other public figure in the world, naming Napoleon as the runner-up. With the surge of Lincoln books that came at the bicentennial of his birth—more than seven hundred books between 2007 and 2011—Lincoln surely has secured his lead in the pantheon of heroes. The titles that follow are among those that ensure his place in history. Only space prevents a more comprehensive listing.

The Lincoln Anthology: Great Writers on His Life and Legacy from 1860 to Now (Library of America, 2008), edited by Harold Holzer, is one of the best books released in recent years and one of the best ever from this invaluable publisher. The nearly one-thousand-page anthology, which includes 110 selections from 95 writers, is a treasure trove of words about Abraham Lincoln—not just from Americans like Ralph Waldo Emerson and E. L. Doctorow but from Karl Marx, Winston Churchill, Henrik Ibsen, Victor Hugo, Bram Stoker, Leo Tolstoy, and H. G. Wells, too. Holzer arranges the excerpts chronologically, from William Cullen Bryant's *Introduction of Abraham Lincoln at*

This bibliography is adapted from the author's "A New Birth of Freedom: Studying the Life of Abraham Lincoln at 200—A Bicentennial Survey," published by *Civil War Book Review*, Spring 2009.

Cooper Union (*New York Evening Post*, February 28, 1860), to E. L. Doctorow's novel *The March* (Random House, 2005). The authors are varied from the famous to the obscure—newspapermen, humorists, biographers, essayists, novelists, memoirists, poets, playwrights, historians, clergymen, and statesmen.

Count S. Stakelberg's contribution to Holzer's anthology quotes Tolstoy as having said of Lincoln, "[O]f all the great national heroes and statesmen of history, Lincoln is the only real giant. Alexander, Frederick the Great, Caesar, Napoleon, Gladstone and even Washington stand in greatness of character, in depth of feeling and in certain moral power far behind Lincoln." Most of the writers agree with Holzer that Lincoln, while complex and self-contradictory, "has remained nothing less than, the ideal American hero: the self-made everyman who triumphed through hard work, unyielding honesty, relentless study, and what Walt Whitman called 'horse-sense.'"[2]

The Portable Abraham Lincoln (Penguin, 2009), edited by Andrew Delbanco, is a collection of Lincoln's most noteworthy speeches, letters, and addresses in a mere 369 pages. In addition to presenting an appropriate selection of Lincoln's key works, Delbanco included a chronology of Lincoln's life. Orville Vernon Burton does the same as editor of *The Essential Lincoln: Speeches and Correspondence* (Hill and Wang, 2009).

Recent short biographies like James M. McPherson's *Abraham Lincoln* (Oxford University Press, 2009) are powerful. This one is 65 pages and complements the more comprehensive biographies as does Allen C. Guelzo's 147-page *Lincoln: A Very Short Biography* (Oxford University Press, 2009).

Brian Lamb and Susan Swain's *Abraham Lincoln: Great American Historians on Our Sixteenth President* (Public Affairs, 2010) contains fifty-five articles about Abraham Lincoln taken from original C-SPAN interviews, giving a virtual biography of America's greatest political leader through the eyes of leading Lincoln historians.

Lincoln was not the most educated president, but he had mastered command of the English language. He was a prolific writer, and his powerful and passionate orations inspired greatness. He was not only a great orator for a set occasion but also a man whose everyday remarks carried enormous verbal power. Without his remarkable ability to communicate with Northerners and Southerners alike, the United States may not have been reunited as one nation. His speeches and writings impart as important a message today as they did nearly two centuries ago. The reading habits that helped Lincoln as an autodidact are shown by Robert Bray's *Reading with Lincoln* (Southern Illinois University Press, 2010) and Daniel Wolff's *How Lincoln Learned to Read* (Bloomsbury, 2010). Both examine training, formal or otherwise, of Lincoln in an effort to identify what makes a good education.

Fred Kaplan's *Lincoln: The Biography of a Writer* (HarperCollins, 2008) is a close study of how crucial Lincoln's vast reading and writing were to his political ascent. In Kaplan's words, "If Mark Twain was the Lincoln of our literature, Lincoln was the Twain of our politics." Indeed, "[s]ince Lincoln, no president has written his own words and addressed his contemporary audience or posterity with equal and enduring effectiveness."[3]

Other books from the bicentennial time examine Lincoln's struggles with race, with his marriage, and with his melancholia. Some cover his law practice, and some investigate his creation of the role of commander in chief.

Lincoln, the Cabinet, and the Generals by Chester G. Hearn (Louisiana State University Press, 2010) provides a comprehensive analysis of Lincoln's complex relationship with both his cabinet and his generals in the field. John C. Waugh also gives a balanced analysis in *Lincoln and McClellan: The Troubled Partnership between a President and His General* (Palgrave Macmillan, 2010), a beautifully written narrative with the president on one side—universally acclaimed and highly respected—and, on the other, a general who is a failure with an ego problem.

Although many of the new releases go down well-beaten paths, they shed new light on the president's life and legacy. Take, for example, Lincoln's epochal 1858 debates about slavery with Senator Stephen A. Douglas of Illinois. In a new edition of the encounters, *The Lincoln-Douglas Debates* (University of Illinois Press, 2008), Rodney O. Davis and Douglas L. Wilson, directors of the Lincoln Studies Center at Knox College, Galesburg, Illinois, do more than any previous studies to reconcile conflicting accounts from rival newspapers. By placing the Lincoln-Douglas debates in historical context, their new work helps the reader understand the full import of the debates, as does Allen C. Guelzo's *Lincoln and Douglas: The Debates That Defined America* (Simon and Schuster, 2009).

Although Douglas kept his Senate seat, Lincoln gained national prominence, leading to an invitation to speak in New York to the eastern Republican establishment. The effect of his speech at the Cooper Union in New York moved him to the forefront of candidates for the Republican nomination for the presidency. In his *Lincoln at Cooper Union*, Holzer (Simon and Schuster, 2006) has written the definitive book on the events surrounding the address.

William Harris's *Lincoln's Rise to the Presidency* (University Press of Kansas, 2007) presents an excellent approach to Lincoln's overall rise in politics leading to his election as president. Harris details Lincoln's development as a politician and leader, demonstrating that although his rise to the presidency was not easy, his journey helped him evolve into a powerful statesman.

Other authors set out to unearth more about Lincoln and his adversaries than earlier scholarship had. In *The Radical and the Republican: Frederick Douglass, Abraham Lincoln, and the Triumph of Anti-Slavery Politics* (Norton, 2008), James Oakes shows that the political foes, although initially ideologically apart on the issue of slavery, grew more similar in their beliefs. Oakes examines two little-noted speeches by Douglass, which reveal that he was more sympathetic than previously thought toward Lincoln's cautious inching toward support for some black suffrage. John Stauffer's insightful *Giants: The Parallel Lives of Fredrick Douglass and Abraham Lincoln* (Twelve, 2008) is a historical essay about two great men and how their relationship grew as a result of Lincoln's gradual acceptance of Douglass's abolitionist positions.

In recent years, many of Lincoln's biographers have taken on the challenge of dissecting Lincoln's mind. For its nuanced view of such key aspects of Lincoln's leadership, Ronald C. White Jr.'s *A. Lincoln: A Biography* (Random House, 2010) has been praised expansively. White's work is lengthy at 797 pages, but his deft writing will appeal to academic and general readers. Stephen B. Oates's classic *With Malice toward None: The Life of Abraham Lincoln* (HarperCollins, 1977) has been reissued by HarperCollins in a revised edition. It is one of the three best biographies of Abraham Lincoln in the last two generations. Benjamin Thomas's *Abraham Lincoln: A Biography* (Knopf, 1952; reissued by Southern Illinois University Press in 2008) and David Donald's *Lincoln* (Simon and Schuster, 1995) round out the trilogy.

Lincoln's long career as a lawyer has become more visible thanks to the enormous project *The Papers of Abraham Lincoln*, undertaken by the Illinois Historic Preservation Agency. The state agency put them into a searchable online database. The agency is responsible, too, for placing *The Collected Works of Abraham Lincoln*, edited by Roy P. Basler and others (Rutgers University Press, 1953), online and updating it, too, along with *Lincoln Day by Day: A Chronology, 1809–1865,* first edited by Earl S. Miers (3 volumes, Lincoln Sesquicentennial Commission, 1960). In 2000, the University of Illinois Press published on DVD the papers from Lincoln's legal practice. Mark E. Neely Jr.'s *Lincoln Encyclopedia* (McGraw-Hill, 1982) remains an indispensable guide as does the more recent *The Political Lincoln: An Encyclopedia*, edited by Paul Finkleman and Martin J. Hershock (CQ, 2009). In another documentation project, *The Lincoln Assassination: The Evidence*, edited by William C. Edwards and Edward Steers Jr., the University of Illinois Press has published the evidence gathered for the Lincoln assassination trials, much of which the court never viewed.

Still, with the record and scholarship on the sixteenth president already so vast, can we expect such delving to bring in major revisions of the Lincoln story?

In *Lincoln President-Elect: Abraham Lincoln and the Great Secession Winter 1860–1861* (Simon and Schuster, 2009), Holzer makes a compelling case that the president-elect was no ditherer but, rather, shrewd and principled as he waged war to prevent Southern secession and end slavery.

Of particular interest is *Lincoln's Men: The President and His Private Secretaries*, by Daniel Mark Epstein (HarperCollins, 2009), which gives an up-close and personal look at the president through the men who knew him best. Of the three secretaries to serve during Lincoln's presidency, the best-known is John Hay, who later became a successful diplomat and Cleveland businessman. In crisp and occasionally wry prose, Epstein shows how Lincoln was perceived by those closer to him than anyone outside his immediate family.

Lincoln's attitude toward African Americans is still a contested matter among authors—many believe the epithet of Great Emancipator is well earned, but some consider him a racist. In a thoughtful introduction to *Lincoln on Race and Slavery* (Princeton, 2009), Henry Louis Gates Jr. details the steady evolution of Lincoln's thinking from his early opposition to slavery on economic rather than humanitarian grounds to arguing, in the last speech of his life, that at the very least black men should have the right to vote. Along these lines, Eric Foner's belief that the hallmark of Lincoln's greatness was his "capacity for growth" fills out *The Fiery Trial: Abraham Lincoln and American Slavery* (Norton 2010).[4]

In 1922, Robert R. Moton, Booker T. Washington's successor at Tuskegee Institute, drafted a speech on behalf of black Americans for the dedication of Washington's Lincoln Memorial, warning that the memorial would remain "but a hollow mockery, a symbol of hypocrisy, unless we together can make real the principles for which

Lincoln died." Though the Memorial Commission ultimately forced Moton to excise his sharp words, his May 30, 1922, speech nevertheless ended with a cry for "equal justice and equal opportunity for all."[5]

The legacy of Abraham Lincoln is measured not only in his deeds but also his words. Lincoln's masterful speechwriting while in office forever changed the way politicians communicate with their constituents.

For *In Lincoln's Hand*, edited by Joshua Wolf Shenk and Harold Holzer (Bantam, 2009), a panel of writers, artists, and past presidents of the United States were each assigned one of Lincoln's original writings and asked to write a commentary on it. An examination of the president's word choice and sentence structure demonstrates how Lincoln used common language—often one- and two-syllable words—to reach a broader audience.

While in New Salem, Illinois, Lincoln began to study law on his own. He passed the Illinois bar examination in 1836 and left to work as a lawyer in Springfield. Over the next twenty-four years, primarily through his work on the Eighth Judicial Circuit, he became one of the most respected attorneys in central Illinois. Much of Lincoln's approach to his later actions as President of the United States was grounded in his hands-on experience with the law. *Lincoln the Lawyer* (University of Illinois Press, 2008), by Brian Dirck, gives a realistic view of what it was like to be a lawyer in Illinois at that time. And Mark Steiner, in *An Honest Calling: The Law Practice of Abraham Lincoln* (Northern Illinois University Press, 2009), tells us that Lincoln the lawyer was busy and supported alternative dispute resolution—mediation—before that term was invented. Most relevant for today's leadership challenges are *Lincoln's Constitution* by Daniel Farber (University of Chicago Press, 2003) and Mark E. Neely Jr.'s *Lincoln and the Triumph of the Nation: Constitutional Conflict in the American Civil War* (University of North Carolina Press, 2011).

For the Civil War, there is no end, and a new crop of books marks its 150th anniversary. Douglas R. Egerton's *Year of Meteors: Stephen*

Douglas, Abraham Lincoln, and the Election That Brought on the Civil War (Bloomsbury, 2010) and Michael Green's *Lincoln and the Election of 1860* (Southern Illinois University Press, 2011) present thorough analyses about the contest that featured four candidates—John C. Breckinridge of Kentucky, nominee of the Southern Democrats; Stephen A. Douglas of Illinois, candidate of the Northern Democrats; John Bell of Tennessee of the Constitutional Union Party; and Abraham Lincoln of the Republican Party.

Has any wartime leader ever spent so much time thinking about the sacrifices of the dead and their meaning? Two books describing Lincoln's role as commander in chief are James M. McPherson's *Tried by War: Abraham Lincoln as Commander in Chief* (Penguin, 2008) and Craig B. Symonds's *Lincoln and His Admirals* (Oxford University Press, 2008). William C. Davis's *Lincoln's Men: How President Lincoln Became Father to an Army and a Nation* (Free Press, 1999) is indispensable to understanding Lincoln's military leadership from the time he served as a volunteer in the Black Hawk War. Lincoln's words relating to war and the military have been collected by Holzer in *Lincoln on War: Our Greatest Commander-in-Chief Speaks to America* (Algonquin Books of Chapel Hill, 2011).

The best description of the administrative acumen of the president is still Doris Kearns Goodwin's classic *Team of Rivals* (Simon and Schuster, 2005). This is a superb collective biography of Lincoln and his major cabinet members and their families. Most members of the Lincoln administration have biographies of their own as well.

Lincoln's dealings with the Supreme Court were important, especially because he needed the court's approval to uphold many of the questionable actions he took to hold the nation together during the Civil War. Brian McGinty analyzes Lincoln's relations with the court in detail in *Lincoln and the Court* (Harvard University Press, 2008). Harvard also published his *Body of John Merryman: Abraham Lincoln and the Suspension of Habeas Corpus* (2011), the president's first constitutional crisis and his bout with Chief Justice Roger B. Taney.

The most important, controversial, and far-reaching document President Lincoln issued was the Emancipation Proclamation. *The Emancipation Proclamation: Three Views (Social, Political, Iconographic)*, by Holzer, Edna Greene Medford, and Frank J. Williams (Louisiana State University Press, 2006), *Lincoln's Emancipation Proclamation: The End of Slavery in America*, by Allen C. Guelzo (New York: Simon and Schuster, 2004), *Lincoln and Freedom: Slavery, Emancipation, and the Thirteenth Amendment*, edited by Harold Holzer and Sara Vaughn Gabbard (Southern Illinois University Press, 2007), Burrus Carnahan's *Act of Justice: Lincoln's Emancipation Proclamation and the Law of War* (University Press of Kentucky, 2007), and Brian Dirck's edited collection *Lincoln Emancipated* (Northern Illinois University Press, 2007), give fair, up-to-date reviews of Lincoln's attitudes toward race and his act of emancipation demonstrating his great political courage.

An offshoot of Lincoln's moral approach to slavery has been an upsurge in interest in Lincoln's overall approach to religion, resulting in several recent books, including Michael Burkhimer's *Lincoln's Christianity* (Westholme, 2007), George Rable's *God's Almost Chosen People: A Religious History of the American Civil War* (University of North Carolina Press, 2010), and Grant N. Havers, *Lincoln and the Politics of Christian Love* (University of Missouri Press, 2009).

Several scholars have recently compiled books on Lincoln's writings and unique way of expressing his thoughts. Examples include Douglas L. Wilson's *Lincoln's Sword: The Presidency and the Power of Words* (Knopf, 2006) and Ronald C. White Jr.'s *The Eloquent President: A Portrait of Lincoln through His Words* (Random House, 2005).

Lincoln's Gettysburg Address and his second inaugural address have also received particular attention in recent years. Gabor Boritt's *Gettysburg Gospel: The Lincoln Speech That Nobody Knows* (Simon and Schuster, 2006) and A. E. Elmore's *Lincoln's Gettysburg Address: Echoes of the Bible and the Book of Common Prayer* (Southern Illinois University Press, 2009) are a definitive appraisal of the speech and its impact. Ron White does the same for Lincoln's second inaugural address in his *Lincoln's Greatest Speech* (Simon and Schuster, 2006) as does James Tackach in *Lincoln's Moral Vision: The Second Inaugural Address* (University Press of Mississippi, 2002).

Librarians should also be aware of the recent availability of Lincoln's speeches and letters in electronic format. The Library of Congress has long had the largest collection of Lincoln's writings and has published fragments from them over the years. The Library of Congress National Digital Library Program and the Manuscript Division published their Abraham Lincoln Papers in digital format at *Abraham Lincoln: A Resource Guide* (www.loc.gov/rr/program/bib/presidents/lincoln/external.html). All of the works contained in this database are searchable by keyword, lending tremendous aid to researchers and authors alike.

Lincoln hagiography—always a high American art—also rose to new levels over the years. Whether it is through art, books, or iconography, Americans cannot get enough of Lincoln. They cannot stop arguing about what made Lincoln great, what he would have done if he had not been assassinated six weeks into his second term, what he would do if he were alive today. Each year, millions of visitors mount the steps of the Lincoln Memorial, gaze at the statue of this American Zeus, and read his immortal words, carved into the walls.

Lincoln, he of the scraggly beard, skinny build, wrinkled brow, and rhetorical radiance, surely has inspired more artists than any other American president. He has been immortalized in every medium from copper to cardboard. He shows up in the film *The Wizard of Oz*. He is the subject of powerful novels and incisive biographies. In *Lincoln in American Memory* (Oxford University Press, 1994), Merrill D. Peterson traced the way Lincoln's image—that craggy profile with its tousled hair and heavy brow—has graced everything from car dealerships to mattress ads.

David Acord's *What Would Lincoln Do?* (Sourcebooks, 2009) is a primer on how Lincoln was able to handle difficult situations that are relevant to today—a lazy relative, lack of civility, and work ethic. How should a person respond to such a situation?

Yet, as we celebrated his two hundredth birthday, the monolithic, mythic Lincoln—the barefoot boy who studied by candlelight and became "honest Abe," "the rail splitter"—is fragmented into an array of competing and contrasting Lincolns. Some are verifiable, others are theoretical, and a few are wholly compatible with the Lincoln of sainted memory. Revisionists have gathered evidence to describe Lincoln the racist, Lincoln the tyrant, Lincoln the crybaby. There are scholars who argue that Lincoln probably was gay, or an atheist, or depressed, or henpecked.

Some authors simply do not favor our sixteenth president. Larry Tagg's *Unpopular Mr. Lincoln: The Story of America's Most Reviled President* (Savas Beatie, 2009) overwhelms the reader with over 473 pages that emphasize the most negative aspects of political rhetoric in American history and does so in a very organized chronological manner. It demonstrates how Lincoln had to have tough skin with all of the ridicule, denigration, and slander heaped upon him during his presidency. John Avery Emison's *Lincoln Uber Alles: A Dictatorship Comes to America* (Pelican, 2009) is an anti-Lincoln screed by a member of the Sons of Confederate Veterans. To the author, Lincoln is responsible for all of America's sins—from slavery to the loss of American civil liberties. In the same ilk is *Lincoln's Marxists* by Al Benson Jr. and Walter Donald Kennedy (Pelican, 2011), who claim the European revolutionists of 1848 migrated to America, founded the Republican Party, and tied the Lincoln administration to communism.

Although for years Lincoln and George Washington ran neck and neck when historians ranked the greatest presidents, lately Lincoln seems to be pulling ahead; he was number 1 in a London *Times* survey in 2008. A *USA Today*/Gallup Poll taken February 7 and 8, 2009, ranked only Ronald Reagan ahead of Lincoln and John F. Kennedy among presidents Americans consider the greatest. But, for Presidents

Day 2009, C-SPAN released the results of its second Historians Survey of Presidential Leadership on February 15, in which a cross-selection of sixty-five presidential historians ranked the forty-two former occupants of the White House on ten attributes of leadership. As in C-SPAN's first such survey, released in 2000, Abraham Lincoln received top billing among the historians. George Washington placed second, while spots three through five were held by Franklin D. Roosevelt, Theodore Roosevelt, and Harry Truman. This political phenomenon is aptly described in *The Leaders We Deserved and a Few We Didn't*, by Alvin Stephen Feezenberg (Basic Books, 2008), who rethinks the presidential rating game. "President Lincoln's political, constitutional, and wartime legacy has transformed American history. He had accepted war to preserve the Union, and with war, to free the slaves," says Lewis E. Lehrman (286), a former Republican candidate for governor of New York and author of a new book on Lincoln's major antislavery speech of 1854 in Peoria, Illinois, in which he railed against Stephen A. Douglas and his Kansas-Nebraska Act allowing slavery to come into the territories (*Lincoln at Peoria*, Stackpole Books, 2008).

This new Lincoln seems to be more nuanced and complex than the one to whom the Lincoln Memorial was dedicated in 1922 and whom Americans have encountered in school, on television, and at the movies. Books of essays, such as *Lincoln Lessons: Reflections on America's Greatest Leader*, edited by Frank J. Williams and William D. Pederson (Southern Illinois University Press, 2009) and *The Living Lincoln*, edited by Thomas A. Horrocks, Harold Holzer, and Frank J. Williams (Southern Illinois University Press, 2011), demonstrate this phenomenon.

For internationalists, *Abraham Lincoln without Borders: Lincoln's Legacy outside the United States*, edited by Jyotirmaya Tripathy, Surs P. Rath, and William D. Pederson (Pencraft International, 2011); *The Global Lincoln*, edited by Richard Carwardine and Jay Sexton (Oxford University Press, 2011); and Amanda Foreman's *World on Fire:*

Britain's Crucial Role in the American Civil War (Random House, 2011) are helpful in understanding Lincoln in a global context.

According to Edna Greene Medford, who served on the Abraham Lincoln Bicentennial Foundation and was one of the judges in a recent C-SPAN poll, "Lincoln continues to rank at the top in all categories because he is perceived to embody the nation's avowed core values: integrity, moderation, persistence in the pursuit of honorable goals, respect for human rights, compassion; those who collect near the bottom are perceived as having failed to uphold those values."[6] William Lee Miller's companion volumes, *Lincoln's Virtues: An Ethical Biography* (Random House, 2002) and *President Lincoln* (Knopf, 2008), beautifully narrate Lincoln's character and the ethical conundrums he confronted.

When asked to write about himself, Lincoln penned only a thin, two-page autobiography. "There is not much of it, for the reason, I suppose, that there is not much of me," said Lincoln, a picture of unsurpassed modesty.[7] Authors today see it differently. Over sixteen thousand books and pamphlets, including about two thousand for children, have been written about Abraham Lincoln, yet writers are not deterred from adding to the collection of information about America's sixteenth and greatest president. One reason for this phenomenon is that his personal story—the rise from poverty to power—is so quintessentially American that he is perceived as embodying the national myth of the self-made man. We look to him for proof that anyone, however humble their beginnings, can ultimately attain the highest office in the land, what historian Gabor Boritt has called "the right to rise."[8]

This book, then, is about the creation of a mythic figure and about a man who became a hero by accident and, as such, became a victim of his own heroic and selfless acts. He was a hero in the very real sense— resilient, willful for good, approachable, self-taught, and effective in communicating his thoughts and vision for America and the world.

NOTES

Preface

1. Theodore Roosevelt quoted in Candace Millard, *The River of Doubt: Theodore Roosevelt's Darkest Journey* (New York: Broadway, 2005), 18.
2. Alan Brinkley, "The 43 Percent President," *New York Times Magazine*, July 4, 1993, 23.
3. Christopher Reeve, quoted in M. P. Singh, *Quote Unquote* (Darya Ganj: Lotus, 2007), 219.
4. Carl Sandburg, *Abraham Lincoln: The Prairie Years and the War Years* (New York: Sterling, 2007), 427.
5. Abraham Lincoln, "Remarks at Poughkeepsie, New York," February 19, 1861, in *The Collected Works of Abraham Lincoln*, ed. Roy P. Basler (New Brunswick, NJ: Rutgers University Press, 1953), 4:228.
6. Sandburg, *Abraham Lincoln*, 313.
7. James M. McPherson, *We Cannot Escape History: Lincoln and the Last Best Hope of Earth* (Urbana: University of Illinois Press, 1995), 81.
8. Paul Johnson, *Heroes: From Alexander the Great and Julius Caesar to Churchill and de Gaulle* (New York: Harper Collins, 2007), xiv.
9. Lincoln, "Second Inaugural Address," March 4, 1865, *Collected Works*, 8:333.

Introduction

1. Doris Kearns Goodwin, *Team of Rivals: The Political Genius of Abraham Lincoln* (New York: Simon and Schuster, 2005), ix.
2. Count S. Stakelberg, "Tolstoi Holds Lincoln World's Greatest Hero," *New York World*, 1909, 386, 387.
3. James MacGregor Burns, *Leadership* (New York: Harper and Row, 1979), 390.
4. Henry Adams, *The Education of Henry Adams: An Autobiography* (Boston: Houghton Mifflin, 1918), 108.
5. Abraham Lincoln, "To Albert G. Hodges," April 4, 1864, *Collected Works*, 7:282.
6. *Recollected Words of Abraham Lincoln*, comp. and ed. Don E. Fehrenbacher and Virginia Fehrenbacher (Stanford: Stanford University Press, 1996), 498.
7. Abraham Lincoln, "Fourth Debate with Stephen A. Douglas at Charleston, Illinois," September 18, 1858, *Collected Works*, 3:146.
8. Abraham Lincoln, "First Debate with Stephen A. Douglas at Ottawa, Illinois," August 21, 1858, *Collected Works*, 3:16; *Collected Works*, 3:145.
9. Frederick Douglass, Philip Sheldon Foner, and Yuval Taylor, *Frederick Douglass: Selected Speeches and Writings* (Chicago: Hill, 1999), 547.

10. Lincoln, "First Debate," 3:27.

11. Robert Smith, chairman, Charles E. Smith Foundation, "Lincoln Cottage Re-Opening," ceremony, Soldier's Home, Washington, DC, February 18, 2008, C-SPAN Video Library, http://www.c-spanvideo.org/program/Cottag.

12. Abraham Lincoln, "Annual Message to Congress," December 1, 1862, *Collected Works*, 5:537.

1. The Prairie Boy from Middle-of-Nowhere, USA

1. Gabor S. Boritt, introduction to *The Lincoln Enigma: The Changing Faces of an American Icon*, ed. by Boritt (Oxford: Oxford University Press, 2001), xxiv.

2. William E. Bartelt, *There I Grew Up: Remembering Abraham Lincoln's Indiana Youth* (Indianapolis: Indiana Historical Society, 2008), 7.

3. Fehrenbacher and Fehrenbacher, *Recollected Words*, 298.

4. Ronald C. White Jr., *A. Lincoln: A Biography* (New York: Random, 2009), 31.

5. Robert Bray, *Reading with Lincoln* (Carbondale: Southern Illinois University Press, 2010), 10.

6. David Herbert Donald, *Lincoln* (New York: Simon and Schuster, 1995), 32.

7. Michael Burlingame, *Abraham Lincoln: A Life*, 2 vols. (Baltimore: Johns Hopkins University Press, 2008), 1:42.

8. Bray, *Reading with Lincoln*, 4.

9. Abraham Lincoln, "'A House Divided': Speech at Springfield, Illinois," June 16, 1858, *Collected Works*, 2:461.

10. William Grimshaw, *History of the United States*, 2nd ed. (Philadelphia: Wanner, 1821), 271.

11. Bray, *Reading with Lincoln*, 4–7.

12. Donald, *Lincoln*, 30.

13. Fred Kaplan, *Lincoln: The Biography of a Writer* (New York: Harper Collins, 2008), 18.

14. Catherine Clinton, *Mrs. Lincoln: A Life* (New York: Harper Collins, 2009), 63–67.

15. Donald, *Lincoln*, 29.

16. Kaplan, *Lincoln*, 7.

17. Anthony Gross, *Lincoln's Own Stories* (La Vergne, TN: Fredonia, 2001), 12.

18. Donald, *Lincoln*, 27.

19. White, *A. Lincoln*, 38.

20. James M. McPherson, *Tried by War: Abraham Lincoln as Commander in Chief* (New York: Penguin, 2008), 3.

2. Lincoln as a Lawyer: The Foundation of a Hero

1. Lincoln, "First Debate," 3:14; *Dred Scott v. Sandford*, 60 U.S. 393 (1857), 407.

2. White, *A. Lincoln*, 38.

3. Frank J. Williams, *Judging Lincoln* (Carbondale: Southern Illinois University Press, 2002), 36.

4. Adam Gopnik, "Angels and Ages: Lincoln's Language and Its Legacy," *New Yorker*, 83, May 28, 2007, 30.

5. John J. Duff, *A. Lincoln: Prairie Lawyer* (New York: Bramhall, 1960), 168.

6. Brian Dirck, *Lincoln the Lawyer* (Urbana: University of Illinois Press, 2007), 106–7.

7. Duff, *A. Lincoln*, 168.

8. Johnson, *Heroes*, 169.

9. Allen D. Spiegel, *A. Lincoln, Esquire: A Shrewd, Sophisticated Lawyer in His Time* (Macon, GA: Mercer University Press, 2002), 57.

10. Lawrence Weldon quoted in ibid.

11. William H. Herndon and Jesse W. Weik, *Herndon's Lincoln*, ed. Douglas E. Wilson and Rodney O. Davis (Urbana: University of Illinois Press, 2006), 210.

12. Leonard Swett quoted in Donald, *Lincoln*, 149.

13. John Littlefield quoted in Roger Billings and Frank. J. Williams, *Abraham Lincoln, Esq.: The Legal Career of America's Greatest President* (Lexington: University Press of Kentucky, 2010), 176.

14. Dirck, *Lincoln the Lawyer*, 43.

15. Henry C. Whitney to Jesse W. Weik, in *Herndon's Lincoln*, 273.

16. Dirck, *Lincoln the Lawyer*, 146.

17. John G. Nicolay and John Hay, *Abraham Lincoln: A History*, vol. 1 (New York: Century, 1890), 150.

18. Emanuel Hertz, *Lincoln Talks: A Biography in Anecdote* (New York: Viking, 1939), 58.

19. Ida Minerva Tarbell, *Boy Scouts' Life of Lincoln* (New York: Macmillan, 1921), 87.

20. *Lincoln Day by Day: A Chronology 1809–1865*, ed. Earl Schenk Miens (Washington, DC: Lincoln Sesquicentennial Commission, 1960), 202, 231.

21. Spiegel, *A. Lincoln, Esquire*, 60.

22. Henry C. Whitney to Jesse Weik, in Douglas T. Wilson, *Herndon's Informants: Letters, Interviews, and Statements about Abraham Lincoln* (Urbana: University of Illinois Press, 1998), 732.

23. Duff, *A. Lincoln*, 169.

24. Dirck, *Lincoln the Lawyer*, 113.

25. Mark E. Steiner, *An Honest Calling* (DeKalb: Northern Illinois University Press, 2006), 87.

26. James C. Conkling, speech to the Chicago Bar Association, January 12, 1851, in *Lincoln among His Friends*, ed. Rufus Wilson Rockwell (Caldwell, ID: Caxton, 1942), 107.

27. Edmund Burke, *Burke's Politics: Selected Writings and Speeches of Edmund Burke on Reform, Revolution, and War*, ed. Ross J. S. Hoffman and Paul Levack (New York: Knopf, 1970), 72.

28. Dirck, *Lincoln the Lawyer*, 96–97.

29. Donald, *Lincoln*, 157.

30. Dirck, *Lincoln the Lawyer*, 97.

31. Duff, *A. Lincoln*, 188.

32. Ibid., 118, 297–98, 298–99.

33. Ibid., 298.

34. "Frank M. Johnson Interview," March 16, 1991, Montgomery, Alabama, American Academy of Achievement, http://www.achievement. org/autodoc/page/joh2int-1.

3. Lincoln's Introduction to Politics

1. Lincoln, "To George Robertson," 15 August 1855, *Collected Works*, 2:318.

2. Lincoln, "Address Delivered at the Dedication of the Cemetery at Gettysburg," November 19, 1863, *Collected Works*, 7:23.

3. "Special 175th Anniversary Section, 1860–1869, Gettysburg: 'Great Turning Point in the History of the Rebellion,'" *Providence (RI) Journal*, July 21, 2004, H-09.

4. Gabor Boritt, *The Gettysburg Gospel: The Lincoln Speech That Nobody Knows* (New York: Simon and Schuster, 2006), 161–62.

5. Stephen A. Douglas quoted in Allen C. Guelzo, *Lincoln and Douglas: The Debates That Defined America* (New York: Simon and Schuster, 2008), 75.

6. Lincoln, "Speech at Springfield, Illinois," July 10, 1858, *Collected Works*, 2:513; added emphasis.

7. Lincoln, "First Debate," 3:14; original emphasis.

8. Ibid., 3:29.

9. Lincoln, "Second Debate with Stephen A. Douglas at Freeport, Illinois," August 27, 1858, *Collected Works*, 3:43.

10. Abraham Lincoln, *The Lincoln-Douglas Debates of 1858*, ed. Edwin Erle Sparks, vol. 3 (Springfield: Illinois State Historical Library, 1908), 592.

11. Lincoln, "First Debate," 3:27.

4. Finding a Hero in a Military Neophyte

1. Williams, *Judging Lincoln*, 36.

2. Francis Fisher Browne, introduction by John Y. Simon, *The Every-Day Life of Abraham Lincoln* (Lincoln: University of Nebraska Press, 1995), 107.

3. Wilson, *Herndon's Informants*, 9.

4. William C. Davis, *Lincoln's Men: How President Lincoln Became Father to an Army and a Nation* (New York: Free Press, 2000), 9, 10.

5. *Maine to the Wilderness: The Civil War Letters of Private William Lawson, 20th Maine Infantry*, ed. Roderick M. Engert (Orange, VA: North South Trader, 1993), 28.

6. Davis, *Lincoln's Men*, 9.

7. Ibid., 10.

8. James G. Randall, *Lincoln: The Liberal Statesman* (New York: Dodd, Mead, 1947), 33–41.

9. Ibid., 33, 37; Lincoln, "Proclamation Suspending the Writ of Habeas Corpus," September 24, 1862, *Collected Works*, 5:437.

10. McPherson, *Tried by War*, 3.

11. Richard N. Current, *Lincoln and the First Shot* (Philadelphia: Lippincott, 1963), 149–53.

12. T. Harry Williams, *Lincoln and His Generals* (New York: Vintage, 2011), vii.

13. Lincoln, "President's Special War Order No. 1," January 31, 1862, *Collected Works*, 5:111–12, 5:15, 5:118–19.

14. Gideon Welles, *Diary of Gideon Welles, Secretary of the Navy under Lincoln and Johnson*, ed. Howard K. Beale, 3 vols. (New York: Norton, 1960), 1:105, 229.

15. David Halberstam, *The Coldest Winter: America and the Korean War* (New York: Amateurs, 2007), 603–4.

16. White, *A. Lincoln*, 497–98.

17. George B. McClellan, *The Civil War Papers of George B. McClellan: Selected Correspondence 1860–1865*, ed. Stephen W. Sears (New York: Ticknor and Fields, 1989), 344–45.

18. John Nicolay to John Hay, October 26, 1862, John G. Nicolay Papers, Library of Congress, Washington, DC.

19. Lincoln, "To George McClellan," October 24, 1862, *Collected Works*, 5:474.

20. McClellan, *Civil War Papers*, 520.

21. Lincoln, "To Henry W. Halleck," October 16, 1863, *Collected Works*, 6:518.

22. Lincoln quoted in Alexander K. McClure, *Abraham Lincoln and Men of War-Times* (Philadelphia: Times, 1892), 196.

23. Carl von Clausewitz, *On War*, ed. and trans. Michael Howard and Peter Paret (1832; Princeton: Princeton University Press, 1976), 87.

5. Courage to Undertake These Extraconstitutional Measures

1. Isaiah Berlin, *The Hedgehog and the Fox: An Essay on Tolstoy's View of History* (New York: Simon and Schuster, 1966), 1.

2. James M. McPherson, "The Hedgehog and the Foxes," *Abraham Lincoln and the Second American Revolution* (New York: Oxford University Press, 1990), 113–14.

3. Lincoln, "Address Delivered at the Dedication of the Cemetery at Gettysburg," November 19, 1863, *Collected Works*, 7:23.

4. Lincoln, "Speech to the One Hundred Sixty-Fourth Ohio Regiment," August 18, 1864, *Collected Works*, 7:505.

5. Lincoln, "Proclamation Calling Militia and Convening Congress," April 5, 1861, *Collected Works*, 4:430; *Abraham Lincoln: A Documentary Portrait Through His Speeches and Writings*, ed. Don E. Fehrenbacher (Palo Alto: Stanford University Press, 1964), 160–62.

6. Daniel Farber, *Lincoln's Constitution* (Chicago: University of Chicago Press, 2003), 16.

7. "Startling from Baltimore: The Northern Troops Mobbed and Fired Upon—The Troops Return the Fire—Four Massachusetts Volunteers Killed and Several Wounded—Several of the Rioters Killed," *New York Times*, April 19, 1861, in *Lincoln in the Times: The Life of Abraham Lincoln as Originally Reported in The New York Times*, ed. David Herbert Donald and Harold Holzer (New York: New York Times, 2005), 110–11.

8. Frank J. Williams, *Abraham Lincoln and Civil Liberties: Then and Now—The Southern Rebellion and September 11*, NYU Annual Survey of American Law 60 (2004): 466. See also Michael Lind, *What Lincoln Believed: The Values and Convictions of America's Greatest President* (New York: Random, 2004), 174.

9. "Startling from Baltimore," 110–11; Williams, *Abraham Lincoln and Civil Liberties*, 466; Lind, *What Lincoln Believed*, 174; William H. Rehnquist, *All the Laws but One* (New York: First Vintage, 1998), 22; Lincoln, "Annual Message to Congress," 5:518, 524.

10. Lincoln, "Order to General Winfield Scott," April 27, 1861, *Collected Works*, 4:344.

11. William H. Rehnquist, *All the Laws but One: Civil Liberties in Wartime* (New York: Knopf, 1998), 23; "A Day with Governor Seward at Auburn," in F. B. Carpenter, *Seward Papers 6634* (July 1870).

12. Lincoln, "Order to General Winfield Scott," 4:344.

13. William F. Duker, *A Constitutional History of Habeas Corpus* (Santa Barbara, CA: Greenwood, 1980), 146.

14. Lind, *What Lincoln Believed*, 174.

15. *Lincoln in the Times*, 117.

16. Richard A. Posner, *Not a Suicide Pact: The Constitution in a Time of National Emergency* (Oxford: Oxford University Press, 2006), 45.

17. Mark E. Neely Jr., *The Fate of Liberty: Abraham Lincoln and Civil Liberties* (Oxford: Oxford University Press, 1991), xvi; Posner, *Not a Suicide*

Pact, 85–86; B. F. McClerren, op-ed, "Lincoln's Actions May Apply to Current War," *Times-Courier* (Charleston, IL), November 19, 2001.

18. Lincoln, "Speech to Special Session of Congress," July 4, 1861, *Collected Works*, 4:430–31.

19. Ibid. See also James M. McPherson, *This Mighty Scourge: Perspectives on the Civil War* (Oxford: Oxford University Press, 2007), 211.

20. Act of August 6, 1861, ch. 63, sec. 3, 12 Stat. 326 (1861). See also Brian McGinty, *Lincoln and the Court* (Cambridge, MA: Harvard University Press, 2008), 29.

21. Richard A. Posner, "The Truth about Our Liberties," in *Rights vs. Public Safety after 911: America in the Age of Terrorism*, ed. Amitai Etzioni and Jason H. Marsh (Lanham, MD: Rowman and Littlefield, 2003), 27.

22. Lincoln, "Message to Congress in Special Session," July 4, 1861, *Collected Works* 4:429.

23. Duker, *Constitutional History of Habeas Corpus*, 147.

24. Ex parte Merryman, 17 F. Cas. 144, 147 (C.C.D. Md. 1861); Brian McGinty, *The Body of John Merryman: Abraham Lincoln and the Suspension of Habeas Corpus* (Cambridge, MA: Harvard University Press, 2011), 73.

25. Arthur T. Downey, "The Conflict between the Chief Justice and the Chief Executive: *Ex parte Merryman*," *Journal of Supreme Court History* 31, no. 3 (2006): 262, 262–78.

26. *Ex parte Merryman*, 17 F. Cas., 145, 147.

27. Downey, "Conflict," 262–78.

28. *Merryman*, 17 F. Cas., 147.

29. Carl B. Swisher, *The Oliver Wendell Holmes Devise: History of the Supreme Court of the United States* (Cambridge: Cambridge University Press, 1974), 848.

30. Farber, *Lincoln's Constitution*, 17. See also Jeffrey Rosen, *The Supreme Court: The Personalities and Rivalries that Defined America* (New York: Times, 2007), 12.

31. McGinty, *Lincoln and the Court*, 4.

32. Lincoln, "Letter to Edward Bates," May 30, 1861, *Collected Works*, 4:390; McGinty, *Body of John Merryman*, 104–7.

33. *Official Opinions of the Attorney General of the United States, Advising the President and Heads of Departments in Relation to their Official Duties* (Morrison, 1868), 10:81.

34. Lincoln, "Letter to Henry W. Halleck," December 2, 1861, *Collected Works*, 5:35; Lincoln, "Proclamation Suspending the Writ of Habeas Corpus," September 24, 1862, *Collected Works*, 5:436–37; Lincoln, "Proclamation Suspending Writ of Habeas Corpus," September 15, 1863, *Collected Works* 6:451–52; Farber, *Lincoln's Constitution*, 159.

35. Lincoln, "Speech to Special Session of Congress," 4:430.

36. Habeas Corpus Act, ch. 80, 12 Stat. 755 (1863).

37. "Civil War Battle Statistics, Commanders, and Causalities," American-CivilWar.com, accessed April 15, 2012, http://www.americancivilwar.com/cwstats.html.

38. Lincoln, "Proclamation Suspending the Writ of Habeas Corpus," September 24, 1862, *Collected Works*, 5:436–37.

39. See also Michael Kent Curtis, "Lincoln, Vallandigham, and Anti-War Speech in the Civil War," 7 *Wm. & Mary Bill of Rights Journal* 7, no. 1. (1998): 105, 119.

40. *War of the Rebellion: A Compilation of the Official Records of the Union and Confederate Armies*, 128 vols. (Washington, DC: GPO, 1880–1901), series 2, 5:480, 485; series 1, 9:380.

41. Ben Perley Poore, *The Life and Public Services of Ambrose E. Burnside, Solider—Citizen—Statesman* (Providence: Reid, 1882), 208–9.

42. Cong. Globe, 37th Cong., 1st Sess. 57–59 (1861). See also Frank L. Klement, *The Limits of Dissent* (Bronx: Fordham University Press, 1998).

43. Ex parte Vallandigham, 68 U.S. 243, 244 (1864).

44. Curtis, "Lincoln, Vallandigham," 105, 107, 122. See also "Vallandigham Arrested," *Atlas & Argus* (Albany, NY), May 6, 1863.

45. Curtis, "Lincoln, Vallandigham," 107.

46. Poore, *Life and Public Services of Ambrose E. Burnside*, 208; Rehnquist, *All the Laws but One*, 65–66.

47. Ex parte Vallandigham, 68 U.S. at 244. See also Curtis, "Lincoln, Vallandigham," 105, 121.

48. *Atlas & Argus* (Albany, NY), May 13, 1863.

49. *The Trial of Hon. Clement L. Vallandigham by a Military Commission and the Proceedings under his Application for a Writ of Habeas Corpus in the Circuit Court of the United States for the Southern District of Ohio* (Cincinnati: Rickey and Carroll, 1863), 33, 37–39.

50. Vallandigham, 68 U.S. at 251.

51. "Lincoln to Erastus Corning and Others," June 12, 1863, *Collected Works*, 6:266.

52. "Revival of Arbitrary Arrests," *Atlas & Argus* (Albany, NY), May 12, 1863.

53. "The Vallandigham Outrage: Meeting at the Capitol in Behalf of Personal Freedom," *Atlas & Argus* (Albany, NY), May 16, 1863.

54. Ibid.; "The Arrest of Vallandigham," *Atlas & Argus* (Albany, NY), May 8, 1863, 2; "Vallandigham Outrage."

55. "General News," *New York Times*, May 19, 1863.

56. "Vallandigham Outrage."

57. "Vallandigham Indignation Meeting at Albany, Letter from Gov. Seymour—An Attempt Made to Break Up the Meeting," *New York Times*, May 17, 1863.

58. "Vallandigham Outrage."

59. "The Vallandigham Outrage: The Voice of the People," *Atlas & Argus* (Albany, NY), May 26, 1863.

60. "The Union Must and Shall Be Preserved," *Albany (NY) Evening Journal*, May 19, 1863. See also "The Great War Meeting," *Albany (NY) Evening Journal*, May 21, 1863.

61. "The Vallandigham Meeting," *Albany (NY) Evening Journal*, May 18, 1863.

62. "Lincoln to Erastus Corning and Others," 6:260–69.

63. Welles, *Diary*, 5 June 1863, 1:223.

64. Lincoln, "To Erastus Corning and Others," 6:265.

65. Ibid., 266.

66. "Revival of Arbitrary Arrests."

67. "Lincoln to Erastus Corning and Others," 6:265, 266–67.

68. Ibid., 264.

69. Phillip Shaw Paludan, "'The Better Angels of Our Nature': Lincoln, Propaganda, and Public Opinion in the North During the Civil War," in *On the Road to Total War: The American Civil War and the German Wars of Unification, 1861–1871*, ed. Stig Forester and Jorg Nagler (Cambridge, MA: German Historical Institute, 1997), 357–76.

70. Lincoln, "First Debate," 3:27.

71. Ex parte Milligan, 71 U.S. 2 (1866).

72. *The Milligan Case*, ed. Samuel Klaus (Holmes Beach, FL: Gaunt, 1997), 64.

73. *Milligan*, 71 U.S. at 106–7.

74. John Yoo, *War by Other Means: An Insider's Account of the War on Terror* (New York: Atlantic Monthly, 2006), 146.

6. The Emancipation Proclamation

1. Lincoln to Albert Hodges, April 4, 1864, *Collected Works*, 7:281.

2. Lincoln, "Second Inaugural Address," March 4, 1865, *Collected Works*, 8:333.

3. Frederick Douglass, *Frederick Douglass: Selected Speeches and Writings*, ed. Philip S. Foner (Chicago: Lawrence Hill, 1999), 491.

4. Lowell Hayes Harrison, *Lincoln of Kentucky* (Lexington: University Press of Kentucky, 2000).

5. Lincoln to Horace Greeley, August 22, 1862, *Collected Works*, 5:389.

6. Ibid., 5:388–89; original emphasis.

7. Mario M. Cuomo and Harold Holzer, eds., *Lincoln on Democracy, His Own Words, with Essays by America's Foremost Civil War Historians* (Bronx, NY: Fordham University Press, 2004), commentary for "A Fit and Necessary Military Measure," 249.

8. Lincoln, "Reply to Emancipation Memorial presented by Chicago Christians of All Denominations, September 13, 1862, *Collected Works*, 5:420.

9. Lincoln, "Emancipation Proclamation," January 1, 1863, *Collected Works*, 6:29.

10. Ibid., 6:30.

11. Lincoln, "Speech at Chicago, Illinois," July 10, 1858, *Collected Works*, 2:501.

12. Lincoln, "Speech at Peoria, Illinois," October 16, 1854, *Collected Works*, 2:247; Lewis E. Lehrman, *Lincoln at Peoria: The Turning Point* (Mechanicsburg, PA: Stackpole, 2008), 126–35.

13. Lincoln, "To James C. Conkling," August 26, 1863, *Collected Works*, 6:408, 409.

14. Wallace Turnage quoted in Randy Kennedy, "I Shall Never Forget the Weeping," in "Slave Journals" and "Ideas and Trends," *New York Times*, June 20, 2004, 14.

15. Charles W. Mitchell, *Maryland Voices of the Civil War* (Baltimore: Johns Hopkins University Press, 2007), 380.

16. Cuomo and Holzer, *Lincoln on Democracy*, 264.

17. Ibid., 265.

18. Lincoln, "Eulogy on Henry Clay," July 6, 1852, *Collected Works*, 2:132.

19. Cuomo and Holzer, *Lincoln on Democracy*, 251.

20. Lincoln, "Address on Colonization to a Deputation of Negros," August 14, 1862, *Collected Works*, 5:371.

21. Lincoln, "Annual Message to Congress," 5:537.

22. Don E. Fehrenbacher, *Lincoln in Text and Context* (Palo Alto: Stanford University Press, 1988), 221.

23. Edward Dicey, *Six Months in the Federal States* (London: Macmillan, 1863), 200.

7. The Assassination and Apotheosis of a Hero

1. Johnson, *Heroes*, xv–xvi.

2. Allan Nevins, *The War for the Union: The Organized War to Victory 1864–1865* (New York: Scribner and Sons, 1959), 319.

3. Carl Sandburg, *Abraham Lincoln: The Prairie Years and the War Years* (New York: Sterling, 2007), 394.

4. Lincoln, "Address before the Young Men's Lyceum of Springfield, Illinois," January 27, 1838, *Collected Works*, 1:109.

5. Harold Holzer, "Abraham Lincoln, American Hero," 2004 Heroes of History Lecture, National Endowment for the Humanities, 2007, accessed April 15, 2012, http://www.myhero.com/myhero/go/specialevents/hero.asp?hero=LBC_HolzerAmericanHero&eid=1.

6. Lincoln, "Second Inaugural Address," 8:333.

7. Ibid.

8. John Wilkes Booth quoted in Michael W. Kauffmann, *American Brutus: John Wilkes Booth and the Lincoln Conspiracies* (New York: Random House, 2004), 399.

9. Kauffman, *American Brutus*, 125.

10. Ward Hill Lamon, *Recollections of Abraham Lincoln, 1847–1865*, ed. Dorothy Lamon Teillard (Chicago: McClurg, 1895), 268.

11. Edward Steers Jr., *Blood on the Moon: The Assassination of Abraham Lincoln* (Lexington: University Press of Kentucky, 2001), 58.

12. Dorothy Meserve Kunhardt and Philip B. Kunhardt Jr., *Twenty Days: A Narrative in Text and Pictures of the Assassination of Abraham Lincoln* (New York: Harper and Row, 1965), 42–49.

13. Thomas Reed Turner, *Beware the People Weeping: Public Opinion and the Assassination of Abraham Lincoln* (Baton Rouge: Louisiana State University Press, 1982), 90.

14. *Illinois State Register* (Springfield, IL), April 15, 1865, 1.

15. U.S. Department of State, *The Assassination of Abraham Lincoln: And the Attempted Assassination of William H. Seward and Frederick W. Seward* (Washington, DC: U.S. Department of the State, 1866), 155.

16. Merrill D. Petersen, *Lincoln in American Memory* (New York: Oxford University Press, 1994), 3–35.

17. David Herbert Donald, "Getting Right with Lincoln," *Harper's Magazine*, April 1951, 74–75.

18. Ibid.

8. A Great American Hero

1. Johnson, *Heroes*, 173.

2. Allen C. Guelzo, *Lincoln's Emancipation Proclamation: The End of Slavery in America* (New York: Simon and Schuster, 2004), 1.

3. Lincoln, "Address Delivered at the Dedication of the Cemetery at Gettysburg," November 19, 1863, *Collected Works*, 7:24.

4. Boritt, *Gettysburg Gospel*, 1200–1201.

5. Carl Sandburg, "Lincoln, Man of Steel and Velvet," *National Geographic*, 117, 1960, 241.

Recent Books on Abraham Lincoln

1. William W. Cook and James Tatum, *African American Writers and Classical Tradition* (Chicago: University of Chicago Press, 2010), 87.

2. Harold Holzer, "Abraham Lincoln: A Legacy Born in Politics," *Organization of American Historians Magazine of History* 23, no. 1 (2009): 7.

3. Fred Kaplan, *Lincoln: The Biography of a Writer* (New York: HarperCollins, 2008), 1.

4. Eric Foner, *The Fiery Trial: Abraham Lincoln and American Slavery* (New York: Norton, 2010), 336.

5. Eric J. Sundquist, *King's Dream* (New Haven, CT: Yale University Press, 2009), 181.

6. Kenneth T. Walsh, "Historians Rank George W. Bush among Worst Presidents, Lincoln and Washington Were Rated as the Best," *U.S. News*, February 17, 2009, accessed April 15, 2012, http://www.usnews.com/news/history/articles/2009/02/17historians-rank-george-w-bush-among-worst-presidents.

7. Sandburg, *Abraham Lincoln*, 161.

8. Gabor Boritt, *Lincoln and the Economics of the American Dream* (Urbana: University of Illinois Press, 1994), 281.

INDEX

Page numbers in italics denote illustrations.

Frank J. Williams, the author or editor of more than fourteen books, is the retired chief justice of the Supreme Court of Rhode Island. He and his wife, Virginia, have amassed a private library and archive that ranks among the nation's largest collections. Williams is the founding chair of the Lincoln Forum and a board member of the Abraham Lincoln Bicentennial Foundation. He is currently at work on an annotated bibliography of all the Lincoln titles published since 1865. Williams also serves as literary editor of the *Lincoln Herald*, where his Lincolniana appears.

**CONCISE
LINCOLN
LIBRARY**

This series of concise books fills a need for short studies of the life, times, and legacy of President Abraham Lincoln. Each book gives readers the opportunity to quickly achieve basic knowledge of a Lincoln-related topic. These books bring fresh perspectives to well-known topics, investigate previously overlooked subjects, and explore in greater depth topics that have not yet received book-length treatment. For a complete list of current and forthcoming titles, see www.conciselincolnlibrary.com.

Other Books in the Concise Lincoln Library

Abraham Lincoln and Horace Greeley
Gregory A. Borchard

Lincoln and the Civil War
Michael Burlingame

Lincoln and the Constitution
Brian R. Dirck

Lincoln and the Election of 1860
Michael S. Green

Lincoln and Medicine
Glenna R. Schroeder-Lein

Lincoln and Race
Richard Striner

Abraham and Mary Lincoln
Kenneth J. Winkle